# ORACLE PL/SQL FOR SQL*FORMS

# ORACLE PL/SQL FOR SQL*FORMS

## An Introduction to PL/SQL for those using SQL*Forms

VERSION 3.0

Alastair E. McCullough

**McGRAW-HILL BOOK COMPANY**

**London** · New York · St Louis · San Francisco · Auckland · Bogotá
Caracas · Lisbon · Madrid · Mexico · Milan · Montreal
New Delhi · Panama · Paris · San Juan · São Paulo
Singapore · Sydney · Tokyo · Toronto

Published by
McGRAW-HILL Book Company Europe
Shoppenhangers Road, Maidenhead, Berkshire, SL6 2QL England
Telephone 0628 23432
Fax 0628 770224

**British Library Cataloguing in Publication Data**
McCullough, Alastair E.
Oracle PL/SQL for SQL Forms: Introduction
for Those Using SQL Forms Version 3.0
I. Title
005.75
ISBN 0–07–707925–6

**Library of Congress Cataloging-in-Publication Data**
McCullough, Alastair E.,
Oracle PL/SQL for SQL *Forms: an introduction for those using
SQL *Forms Version 3.0 / Alastair E. McCullough.
p. cm.
Includes index.
ISBN 0–07–707925–6 :
1. SQL (Computer program language) 2. Oracle (Computer file)
I. Title.
QA76.73.S67M33 1994
005.75′65–dc20 93–48263
CIP


1234 PB 9654

Typeset by TecSet Ltd, Wallington, Surrey
and printed and bound in Great Britain by Page Bros, Norwich

This book is dedicated to R. de B. and J. L. McCullough, and to Ron Reeves, who thought that I should aim higher than I was heading

*Stop boasting of intellect and learning;*
*for here intellect is hampering,*
*and learning is stupidity.*

***Hakim Jami***
(1414 – 1492)

# CONTENTS


Preface xi
Acknowledgements xiii
Conventions xv
Introduction xvii

## PART ONE Introduction to the PL/SQL language for V3-Style Triggers 1

**Chapter One Introducing PL/SQL** **3**
Setting the scene 3
Oracle SQL quiz 4
Quiz solutions 8
PL/SQL and SQL*Forms Version 3 9
PL/SQL: the language 10
Blocks and sections 12
Writing V3 Triggers using PL/SQL 14
Special symbols and characters in PL/SQL 15
Including comments in program code 15
Four types of variables 16
SQL*Forms V3 SYSTEM variables 19
Declaring PL/SQL identifiers: datatypes 19
Example DECLARE section 21
Declaring identifiers: %TYPE 21
Moving data: SELECT...INTO 22
Moving data: mixed examples 23
What happens when different Variable Objects have the same name? 24
Entering a V3 Trigger in SQL*Forms V3 26
Using the compiler and compilation errors form 28
Practical Session One 29

**Chapter Two Cursors** **32**
CURSOR 32
Simple cursors 33
Parameterized cursors 34
OPEN 35
CLOSE—terminating use 36
Designer's notebook: an aside about parsing cursors 37
FETCH...INTO 38
Multiple FETCHES without loops 39
Cursors and explicit cursor attributes 40
Cursors and implicit cursor attributes 41
Attribute action/contents table 42
Iteration: simple or 'infinite' LOOPs and EXIT 43
Looking more closely at EXIT WHEN 44
Iteration: simple FOR loops 45
Iteration: FOR loop rules 46
Conditions: IF...THEN...ELSIF...ELSE 47
IF... conditional tests supported 48
Example IF...THEN...ELSIF...ELSE clauses 48
Branching: GOTO and naming blocks 50
More rules about GOTO 51
Labels in PL/SQL 51
Practical Session Two 52

**Chapter Three Exceptions** **56**
Introduction 56
Declaring user-defined exceptions 57
EXCEPTION section 58
User-Defined EXCEPTION examples 59
Triggering User-Defined Exceptions: RAISE 60
Exception rules 60
The FORM_TRIGGER_FAILURE Exception 62

PART TWO Form-Level and Packaged Procedures, Packaged Functions 65

**Chapter Four FORM-LEVEL PROCEDURES** **67**
Introduction 67
Procedure definition 68
Simple Form-Level Procedures 69
Simple Form-Level Procedures: examples 71
Form-Level Procedures with parameters 72

Parameterized procedure: example 73
Practical Session Three 75

**Chapter Five Packaged Procedures** **78**
Packaged Procedures introduced 78
A reminder about object referencing 79
Trigger types and restrictions table 80
Packaged Procedures' restrictions and overview 82
Key-related Packaged Procedures' restrictions and overview 84
EXECUTE_TRIGGER( ) 85
CALL( ), CALL_QUERY( ) 86
NEW_FORM( ) 87
EXIT_FORM( ) 87
POST 88
CLEAR_FORM( ) 89
COMMIT_FORM 90
CLEAR_BLOCK( ) 90
CLEAR_EOL, CLEAR_FIELD, CLEAR_RECORD 91
DEFAULT_VALUE( ) 92
COPY_REGION, CUT_REGION, PASTE_REGION 92
DISPLAY_FIELD( ) 93
SET_FIELD( ) 94
EDIT_FIELD( ) 95
The art and architecture of Pages 96
Pop-up Pages 96
View Size, Page Size, View Page, and View Loc 98
Page Definition displays 99
Page View control 101
Page Display control 102
Designer tip: automatic pages and SYNCHRONIZE 103
ERASE( ) 104
DO_KEY( ) 105
ENTER_QUERY( ) 105
EXECUTE_QUERY( ) 106
GO_place( ) 108
HOST( ) 108
USER_EXIT( ) 109
LIST_VALUES( ) 110
MESSAGE( ) 110

**Chapter Six Packaged Functions** **112**
Introduction 112
APPLICATION_ and FORM_CHARACTERISTIC 112
FORM_FAILURE, _FATAL, _SUCCESS 113
BLOCK_CHARACTERISTIC( ) 114

FIELD_CHARACTERISTIC( ) 115
ERROR_CODE, _TEXT, and _TYPE 116
Examples of error-testing code 117
MESSAGE_CODE, _TEXT, and _TYPE 118
Examples of message-testing code 119
Using Packaged Procedures and Packaged Function NAME_IN( ) 121
Further indirection with NAME_IN( ) 122
Copy/Reference Object Facility 122
Object referencing restrictions 123
Practical Session Four 125

PART THREE APPENDICES: Data, additional information, addenda 129

Appendix A: Definitions for example work 131
Table definitions for example work 131
Data definitions for example tables 133

Appendix B: Using PL/SQL DML commands 135
Program output: INSERT and assignment 135
Program output INSERT and assignment rules 136
Program output: using UPDATE 137
Program output: using DELETE 138
Transactions: COMMIT and ROLLBACK 139
Transactions: using SAVEPOINTS 140
Example: program using COMMIT 142

Appendix C: Formatting using TO_CHAR( ) 144
Dates: prefixes and suffixes 145

Appendix D: Example Page Attributes' Adjustments 147

Glossary 151

Index 165

# PREFACE

Much of the material contained here originated in a four-day course I wrote for Datacase Corporation in late 1992, 'Oracle SQL*Forms V2.3 to V3.0 Conversion'. I am indebted to the students who attended this and also the subsequent 'PL/SQL for SQL*Forms' course, for their comments, patience, and goodwill.

The motivation behind the course was a major gap in the available non-Oracle Corporation literature on the subject and my desire adequately to teach a way through the SQL*Forms and PL/SQL jungle. It is, for me, an extraordinarily fascinating and wonderful jungle, but it is nevertheless a jungle, and one in which the unwary take their lives in their hands. I continue to make a plea for the inexperienced to take time to learn and learn and learn before they call themselves 'Consultants': even after 40 years, the IT industry is still too full of faith rather than reality.

Alastair McCullough

# ACKNOWLEDGEMENTS

As always, there are all sorts of people to whom my thanks must go for their support in one way or another. Many have inspired teaching approaches or have given me ideas over the past few years: some of these have reacted with one another or formed the basis for further work, all of which has helped in the melting-pot effect. Some people have even been good enough to complain, and so helped me in that way, too.

Thanks, then, for all sorts of reasons, go to Trevor Trotman, Daphne Caldeira, Mustafa Nasrulla, John Styles, John Morris, all those who attended my Oracle Systems Development courses at BT Research Laboratories at Martlesham Heath and the BT Belfast Engineering Centre, and so many other students who have been kind enough to ask illuminating questions, Howard Bradley, my friends at the Institute for Cultural Research, John Radcliffe of Oracle Corporation UK, who suggested in 1992 that I develop and advance PL/SQL specialization at Datacase Corporation, and to my publishers, McGraw-Hill, for their enthusiasm.

# CONVENTIONS

Pages are set out in the following manner. Sometimes, to make the content more readable or visually interesting, slight alterations in the typeface have been used in the body of page information, together with graphics. Generally, Backus Naur Form (BNF) notation has been avoided in order to ensure simplicity and ease of use as a reference work. Purists will complain, but this is a book for practitioners. For commands:

COMMAND and additional syntax
at the top of the page
*Options can be shown in italics.*
[*Where explanation is enhanced,*
*square brackets show options, too.*]

Explanation of the command, syntactical, and operational points will usually be one or more paragraphs of information.

> Fact Box containing key information or highlighting significant points.

- Command rules and usage points;
- Command rules and usage points;
- Command rules and usage points.

```
EXAMPLE
program code is shown in Courier fount
and contains examples using the Parallel Universe
Database (see page xviii);
Sometimes this will be highlighted
to enhance understanding.
```

Some pages include tables for reference:

**Table**

| | |
|---|---|
| Showing and | various items of data information |

# SQL Layout standard

The Oracle industry is bedevilled by many people who refuse to write their SQL code in a sensible and easily readable form. Typically, SQL joins and subqueries are written in a haphazard and utterly confusing way. Throughout this book, an attempt has been made to standardize on a proper SQL layout. This has the major advantage in real-world programming that debugging is simplified; writing is speeded; and understanding is enhanced. Reasons enough for apparent pedantry!

The following general layout has been adopted:

```
SELECT     column_or_expression1 [alias1],
           column_or_expression2 [alias2],
           :
           column_or_expressionn [aliasn]
FROM       table1 [alias1],
           table2 [alias2],
           :
           tablen [aliasn]
WHERE      condition1
AND        condition2
           :
AND        conditionx
OR         condition3
           :
OR         conditionn
GROUP BY   column_or_expression
HAVING     condition
ORDER BY   column_or_expression;
```

This is not to be taken as a precise Backus Naur Form statement of SQL clauses and command options, merely as an indication of layout!

# INTRODUCTION

SQL*Forms Version 3 is the latest widely available release of the SQL*Forms product. It differs markedly from earlier releases because it adds the PL/SQL language capability to Forms, and because many improvements have been made to the operation and appearance of the system, including the ability to provide pop-up windows and on-screen editing capabilities for end-users. Additionally, various new types of trigger (program code) are available in Version 3 that were not in earlier versions. This book is an introduction to all the major features of PL/SQL for use in programming triggers.

In writing the book it has been assumed that the reader has a thorough grounding in Structured Query Language (SQL), often known as 'Sequel', including Data Definition (DDL) and Data Manipulation (DML) sublanguages. Without such a knowledge it is not possible to make any use of Oracle Corporation's PL/SQL language or to understand the concepts behind this book. In addition, the reader is assumed to have a sound knowledge of Oracle's SQL*Forms product in its Version 3.0 release. In particular, a sound grasp of conceptual operations such as those represented by the cursor and Navigation Unit as they move through the runtime Form, initiating sub-events and actuating triggers, is really essential.

It is very important that the reader is aware of some general points. Oracle Corporation's database system is available on a very wide range of different platforms, currently numbering somewhere in the region of a hundred. As with any language, although the majority of PL/SQL, SQL*Forms and SQL commands and facilities usually work in the same way on different equipment, there are always the odd differences that defy explanation. Particularly with a product as extremely complex as Oracle, the combination of PL/SQL and SQL*Forms running on a given platform may not always yield wholly identical results for a given application by comparison with another platform's version: hardware, software, firmware, and airware all combine to provide an ideal breeding ground for confusion and blunder!

Readers are strongly advised to check that commands and approaches suggested here apply on their platform and site. In particular, it is essential always to be at least aware of the release notes supplied by Oracle Corporation for a given product and platform. Any piece of software must be thoroughly tested and debugged before being run with live data: too many times have I heard horror stories reminiscent of the Dark Ages, rather than modern business procedures.

Finally, this book covers PL/SQL for SQL*Forms, and it does not attempt exhaustively to describe the PL/SQL language: that has been left for another book. In particular, there is no discussion of the %ROWTYPE datatype, since developers are assumed to be working in SQL*Forms and making use of the block operations available. Additionally, various constructs are not discussed, neither are WHILE...END LOOP, PRAGMA EXCEPTION_INIT, or explicit locking facilities. This book is not intended to reiterate any Oracle Corporation text, and the reader is referred to the *PL/SQL User's Guide and Reference Version 1.0,* Part No.800-V1.0, April 1989 (revised November 1990) for such information.

## —Parallel Universe Limited—

Some years ago, when I first began to teach Oracle, it became apparent that I would need a company upon whose data I could safely work without causing concern. Parallel Universe Limited was the result. The design criterion was that students always feel happy working with personnel data: it is familiar, even if names are not, all companies need it, and it can easily be invented if necessary!

Parallel Universe Limited is an entirely imaginary company. It seems to be involved in all sorts of different lines of work, and the full company has a number of different tables in its database that can be used by those studying course materials. Principally, Parallel Universe is involved in computer consultancy. It has five divisions: Administration, Consulting, Training, Sales, and Computing. Because it is still a young company, Training and Computing currently have no staff in them.

The full database contains the tables STAFF (personnel data: surnames, salaries, etc.), DIVISION (divisional information: division code, location, name), JOBGROUP (salary grades information), and VEHICLE (company cars data). One of the recently formed functions is Recruitment, and it is the recruitment database that the reader will meet during the course of this book. The recruitment database contains the following tables:

| | |
|---|---|
| CLIENT | Contains data about company clients. |
| PROJECT | Contains information about projects to which recruits are assigned. |
| RECRUIT | Contains personal and salary data for recruits. |
| ASSIGNMENT | Contains recruit project assignments information. |

The initial content and table definitions for Recruitment are contained in Appendix A at the end of this book.

## PL/SQL and Oracle7

The range of Oracle tools, and the Kernel itself, are in a continuous state of change and development at Oracle Corporation. With the advent of Oracle7, the emphasis upon PL/SQL as a development language has become much greater than it was for Oracle Version 6. It has become an important tool for development within the Oracle environment as a whole, rather than just as an element within SQL*Forms.

One of the major innovations in Oracle7 has been the introduction of the CREATE TRIGGER, CREATE PACKAGE and CREATE PROCEDURE commands in Oracle Structured Query Language. This brings PL/SQL within the ambit of the Kernel in a very direct way. For example, a PL/SQL trigger can be fired to perform validation for a given table when rows are inserted. There is a range of event-related triggers that can be programmed by a developer.

The change of emphasis brought about by Oracle7 enhancements can mean adjustments to the way in which projects are completed. For example, there is no need to have a piece of trigger code replicated in each of a series of Forms if that code can be centralized within the database itself, called whenever an INSERT to a table occurs.

Wider questions are raised about the systems development methodology applicable in such a scenario, and about the general strategy and planning associated with any Oracle7 project. As we shall see by the end of this book, there are some surprising repercussions in utilizing the full range of facilities: 'semi-intelligent' code, for example, was possible only with 3GLs until the addition of certain packaged functions (see this section later in the book).

PL/SQL itself is being enhanced, and it is hoped that later editions of this book will include these. The current text has been written, tested, and, as far as possible, debugged using SQL*Forms Version 3.0 and Oracle Kernel Version 6.0. Virtually all the PL/SQL examples have actually been coded and run.

Finally, this book is based upon the original widely released version of PL/SQL, V1.0.32. There are slight differences in the operation of this version by comparison with earlier ones. Where appropriate, I have endeavoured to include relevant notes to support these. PL/SQL Version 2 will not be available for use in SQL*Forms Version 3.0, but new Oracle7 server-side objects, such as Packages can be called from V3-Style Triggers in Version 3.0, according to the latest releases of Oracle Corporation literature.

# PART ONE

# Introduction to the PL/SQL Language for V3-Style Triggers

*There are three ways of presenting anything.*
*The first is to present everything.*
*The second is to present what people want.*
*The third is to present what will serve them best.*
*If you present everything, the result may be a surfeit.*
*If you present what people want, it may choke them.*
*If you present what will serve them best, the worst is that, misunderstanding, they may oppose you. But if you have served them thus, whatever the appearances, you have served them, and you, too, must benefit, whatever the appearances.*

***'Three Ways'***

***Ajmal of Badakhshan***

## CHAPTER ONE

# INTRODUCING PL/SQL

## Setting the scene

At the time of writing, Structured Query Language, or SQL, has been available for business or academic use for nearly two decades. In that time it has proved to be perhaps the most successful and widely known of all the database control and manipulation languages, and has been enshrined in the ANSI SQL89 (SQL2) and ISO 9075 standards. It contains many very powerful constructs, and the combination of functions provided has ensured that it has maintained a position in the database marketplace.

SQL is primarily a Fourth Generation Language, or 4GL. That is, its concepts are firmly founded upon non-procedural lines. It is far more a 'what to' than a 'how to' language, and as such suffers from few of the problems that have traditionally beset the Third Generation (3GL) Programmer, from failure to initialize variables through to the almost inevitable function and subroutine call problems and logical flow complexities that can arise through procedural irregularities prior to successful debugging.

Of course, 3GLs have always proved faster than SQL, not least because of the ease and straightforwardness with which they can be optimized. Oracle Corporation, recognizing both the speed of 3GLs and the need to allow Oracle itself to integrate with existing applications software, provided a range of procedural interfaces and pre-compilers in the form of the Pro*Oracle languages, such as Pro*C, Pro*COBOL, Pro*Fortran, etc. These languages have provided the twin advantages of an already established and tested Query Language in the form of Embedded Structured Query Language (ESQL—very similar to SQL but providing additional host language functionality) and the sound user and programmer base of a range of popular 3GL languages. As the Oracle and SQL applications bases have widened, it has become apparent that Structured Query Language must be either altered or appended to allow for the use of procedural constructs.

# Oracle SQL quiz

*Complete the quiz questions below. Many of them are multiple-choice questions, and you need only tick the solution you think is most likely to be correct. The idea is not to catch you out but to help you to 'warm up' for the PL/SQL and SQL in this book. It is tempting to cheat, but try not to look at the solutions. The idea is to have fun: do not take it too seriously!*

1 Which following construct is illegal?

(a) ORDER BY 3
(b) ORDER BY SURNAME ASC
(c) ORDER BY DESC
(d) ORDER BY JOBTITLE, SURNAME, SALARY
(e) ORDER BY SALARY/12 + POWER(TAX, 2)/12 * 17.5

2 Consider this construct:

```
select surname
from   person  p
where  p.snum in (select v.snum
                  from   vehicle v
                  where  v.snum = p.snum);
```

Its structure in SQL is correctly called

(a) A 'nested query'?
(b) A 'correlated subquery'?
(c) An 'outer join'?
(d) A 'concatenated key'?
(e) A 'sort/merge'?

3 Suppose that the function ROUND(14365.27, -3) is parsed. What will be the output from it?

(a) An error code and report.
(b) 14365.270
(c) 14000
(d) 14000.27
(e) 65.27

4 Correct the following query (look for about 10 errors—you may find more!) by circling, highlighting, and commenting on the errors:

```
SELECT cr.cowner,
       cr.mileage,
FROM   car_rec_inp_det01 cr
WHERE  (cr.engine_size,
       y.regno,
       cr.manufacturer) = (SELECT   k.litres,
                                    k.index_mark,
                           FROM     person_cars k,
                                    user urec
                           WHERE    rp.owner =
                                      "PETTIGREW"
                           ORDER BY urec.sdate)
ORDER BY   y.model;
```

5 What does the pseudo-column ROWNUM contain?

(a) Internal Oracle block and address of each row in a table.
(b) An unique identifier for each row, system-maintained.
(c) The sequential number of the current query output row, if any.
(d) The **R**esource **OW**ner **NU**meric **M**arker identifier for each table.
(e) The unique identifier for the ROLLBACK Segment for this user.

6 What will the result be when this function is parsed?

```
INITCAP('STYLES-FFOOKES')
```

(a) Styles-Ffookes
(b) Styles-FFOOKES
(c) STYLES-ffookes
(d) There will be no output.
(e) styles-ffookes

7 The SYSDATE is set to Wednesday 22 April 1992. Assume that this has been parsed through the following function. What will be the result?

```
TO_CHAR(SYSDATE, 'fmYYdydyYYMonCCCC')
```

(a) 92222292Apr1992
(b) Wed 22 Apr 1992
(c) 20wdwd20mon1992
(d) 92wdwd92Apr2000
(e) 92wedwed92Apr2020

8 Which three of the following general forms are not valid equi-joins?

(a) WHERE a.col = b.col = c.col = d.col
(b) WHERE a.col = b.col AND b.col = c.col
(c) WHERE a.col < > b.col AND b.col < > c.col
(d) WHERE a.col = b.col
(e) WHERE a.col BETWEEN b.col AND c.col

9 For what purpose is the (+) sign used in a join?

(a) Indicates the VIEW from which this column comes.
(b) Indicates the deficient table in an Outer Join.
(c) Invokes a new cursor in Random Access Memory for speed.
(d) Makes any negative numeric datum found into a positive number.
(e) Copies rows from the set returned by a subquery to an outer query.

10 Which one of the following lists correctly states the major Data Definition Language commands available in Oracle SQL?

| (a) | (b) | (c) |
|---|---|---|
| INSERT<br>UPDATE<br>REVOKE | INSERT<br>UPDATE<br>DELETE | CREATE<br>TABLE<br>SELECT |

| (d) | (e) |
|---|---|
| CREATE<br>UPDATE<br>DROP | CREATE<br>ALTER<br>DROP |

11 Which one of the following lists correctly states the major Data Manipulation Language commands available in Oracle SQL?

| (a) | (b) | (c) |
|---|---|---|
| INSERT<br>UPDATE<br>DELETE<br>SELECT | CREATE<br>UPDATE<br>DELETE<br>SELECT | GRANT<br>UPDATE<br>DELETE<br>SELECT |

| (d) | (e) |
|---|---|
| INSERT<br>DELETE<br>SAVEPOINT<br>DROP | GRANT<br>ROLLBACK<br>REVOKE<br>COMMIT |

12 Which two of the following datatypes is not available in standard Oracle SQL?

(a) CHAR(n)
(b) LONG RAW
(c) NUMBER(n)
(d) ALPHANUM(n)
(e) TIME

13 Which is the only correct standard representation for this date in Oracle?

(a) 23-NOV-92
(b) "23-NOV-92"
(c) 23.NOV-92
(d) (23-NOV-92)
(e) '23-NOV-92'

14 Which of the following will store any DML statement's work during the current Transaction (from Oracle Version 6+)?

(a) COMMIT
(b) ROLLBACK
(c) Any DDL command
(d) EXIT
(e) SAVEPOINT

15 As far as you are aware, which of the following functions do not exist?

| | | | |
|---|---|---|---|
| (a) | TO_UPPER( ) | (b) | TRANSLATE( ) |
| (c) | RAWTOHEX( ) | (d) | LAST_DAY( ) |
| (e) | TO_TIME( ) | (f) | NVL( ) |
| (g) | DECODE( ) | (h) | NULL( ) |
| (i) | SOUNDEX( ) | (j) | GOTO( ) |
| (k) | TRUNC( ) | (l) | RETURN |
| (m) | NEW_VALUE( ) | (n) | OLD_VALUE( ) |
| (o) | ABS( ) | (p) | RTRIM( ) |
| (q) | LTRIM( ) | (r) | SUBSTR( ) |
| (s) | ERROR( ) | (t) | RAWVAL( ) |
| (u) | INT( ) | (v) | RND( ) |
| (w) | CHR( ) | (x) | CHR$( ) |
| (y) | SUM( ) | (z) | COUNT( ) |

## Quiz solutions

1 (c) because DESC is a keyword without a column.
2 (b). It is actually a Correlated Subquery because of the inner query referencing the column in the outer table.
3 (c) because the negative number will round the left-hand side of the decimal.
4 (i) Needs another column in the outer query, possibly.
(ii) The DATA may differ between ENGINE_SIZE and LITRES.
They could be the same, though ('INDEX_MARK' is a term used by the police, for example.)
(iii) No ORDER BY allowed in a subquery.
(iv) Table Y has not been defined.
(v) "PETTIGREW" should be in *single quotes*!

(vi) We do not know that 'PETTIGREW' will only return one ROW, hence there might be a '*Single Row subquery returns more than one row*' error.
(vii) Alias RP has not been defined anywhere.
(viii) Left-hand side does not match right-hand side of the subquery.
(ix) Extraneous comma in buffer line 2;
(x) Extraneous comma in buffer line 7.
(xi) An under-specified WHERE clause often yields a Cartesian Product.

5 (c). Like 1, 2, 3, 4, ... 30, ... 234, ... etc.
6 (a). But it cannot cope with names like 'McCullough,' 'MacCrae,' 'de Chesney'...!
7 (e). dy is the abbreviated day. CC, the century. Mon, the abbreviated month.
8 (a) because it is rubbish. (c) because they would never join. (e) because it is not based upon an *equivalency.*
9 (b). Chris Date, the famous Relational writer, points out in one of his voluminous books that it would make more sense to put the Outer Join operator in the FROM clause rather than in the join. I agree with him!
10 (e). Definition Language builds the houses the data will live in.
11 (a). Manipulation Language plays with the data.
12 (d) and (e). The others are quite legal.
13 (e), though sometimes the contents of the single quotes can be jiggled slightly.
14 (a), (c), and (d). Always be wary of EXIT and QUIT commands.
15 (a), (e), (h), (j), (l), (m), (n), (s), (t), (u), (v), (x). SUM( ) and COUNT( ) are group functions, though, not for single rows.

# PL/SQL and SQL*Forms Version 3

Structured Query Language (SQL) is already very powerful, but it suffers from an inability to perform what for 3GL Languages are relatively simple operations: recursive, iterative, and conditional structures that allow repetition of frequently used code. There is an argument which says that Structured Query Language should avoid the use of non-relational operations, since it is alleged that it is possible to perform any required functions using the language as it stands. Pragmatic analysis, though, proves that this is often not the case!

Oracle Corporation have recognized both that a simpler way of programming is required and that a sophisticated batch-processing language should be available that incorporates the elements of procedural processing languages to allow simplicity and ease of construction without an in-depth knowledge of academic Structured Query Language. The solution arrived in the United States with Oracle Version 6, and was called PL/SQL.

In this section we concentrate upon using simple PL/SQL for processing information in SQL*Forms Version 3, not as a standalone batch-processing language. It should be stated clearly here that we will not be covering PL/SQL in depth here. The language, like any other serious computer language, has considerable depth and complexity and requires specialist study for the designer to become completely used to its oddities and abilities.

PL/SQL has good conditional control facilities, rather than requiring the programmer to make use of the SELECT 'x' FROM DUAL construct used as a standard SQL condition test clause, or the V2 CASE macro, which is often too clumsy or requires Byzantine programming. PL/SQL also allows straightforward procedural branching and looping. Previously, branching could only be effected by using Forms Macros or, implicitly, by processing the Failure or Success of a given substep within a trigger program.

SQL*Forms Version 3 enables the designer to build up a library of PL/SQL programs and functions, called 'Forms Procedures', callable from a variety of applications through the use of the Forms 3 object referencing and referential integrity facilities. Triggers in Forms may also be copied between Forms, enforcing still further the idea of a 'library' of routines for use on applications.

## PL/SQL: the language

PL/SQL is based generally around Ada, the language developed for use by the Pentagon in the United States, and indeed, for conceptual study Oracle recommend perusing the US Department of Defense Manual, *Military Standard, Ada Programming Language,* published in 1983. The first PL/SQL reference manual was released in April 1989, though the language itself was unavailable in the United Kingdom in general release form until 1991. PL/SQL is designed to augment Structured Query Language, and cannot operate without it, nor can it function as a standalone product without an associated Oracle Instance.

PL/SQL is used primarily in three major roles: first, as a transaction-processing language in its own right; second, as an embedded language in applications developed using Oracle, in which respect it is very similar to the vast range of Fourth and semi-Fourth Generation Languages; third, as a new programming facility in Oracle's SQL*Forms environment (see Fig. 1.1).

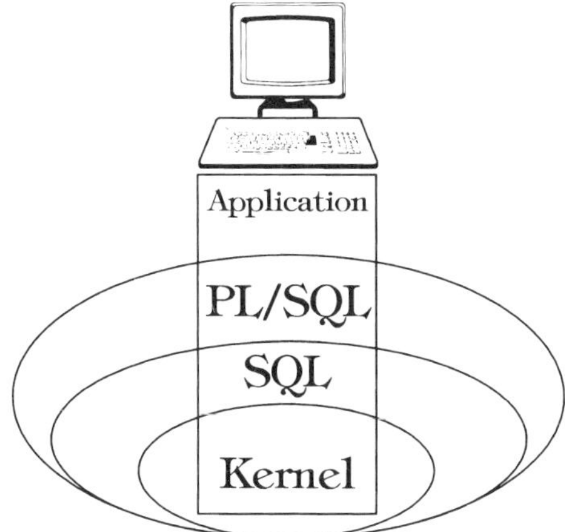


*Figure 1.1 Application of PL/SQL.*

## Transaction processing

As a transaction-processing language, PL/SQL is written in file format and stored similarly to SQL*Plus text files as a series of lines of code. It can be mixed with SQL and SQL*Plus commands, together with documentation text. *Alternatively,* it can be written in SQL*Forms triggers, where SQL*Plus commands are illegal, but there will be a variety of 'packaged procedures' and 'packaged functions' available: special Forms-related functions that can work together with PL/SQL within applications. This approach allows the designer to build up a library of routines that can work together by making use of the START command in SQL*Plus, or can be called singly, or stored within SQL*Forms.

Obviously, very large programs can be written, and the SQL*Plus output and user-interaction commands can be combined so that the whole works in every respect similarly to that of the 'normal' transaction-processing language. Other advantages exist in allowing the code to be shared among applications, between programmers and project teams, and across company-distributed sites. It is worth noting that PL/SQL should be available upon all the platforms on which Oracle Version 6 and Oracle7 will operate, and thus is completely portable across systems.

It is important to emphasize that some functions are available in PL/SQL that are exactly the same as those in SQL in terms of their operation and appearance. However, these are PL/SQL not SQL functions, and will yield PL/SQL errors (if they occur) rather than SQL errors. Additionally, thought must be given to usage where a programmer normally expects more than one value to be returned as the result of a query.

### Embedded program code

PL/SQL can be embedded in host languages by making use of the Pro*Oracle Pre-compilers and procedural interfaces, Pro*C, Pro*Ada, Pro*COBOL, Pro*Fortran, Pro*Pascal, and Pro*PL/1, together with ESQL commands, which differ slightly from the non-embedded version by virtue of the fact that they contain current record pointers and allow the ability to interact with host variables, for example.

## Blocks and sections

```
DECLARE
        declarative statements...
BEGIN
        executable statements...
EXCEPTION
        exception handler statements...
END;
```

A PL/SQL program is known as a 'block', short for 'block of code'. The term allows for its use both as an independent program and as a series of statements included in a host language.

A block may begin with either DECLARE or BEGIN, but it *must* start with one or the other.

## DECLARE

This name is given to a section of the block in which any variables, constants, or other special objects that will be used in the block are defined. Variables and constants must always be defined before they can be used in PL/SQL: unlike some other languages, PL/SQL does not support the inclusion of undeclared variables. Although this may seem annoying, it does ensure that each program has a known structure and makes logical sense. There are also positive gains from readability and ease of planning. Objects other than variables and constants are discussed elsewhere in this book.

## BEGIN

Generally, there should always be a BEGIN statement at the start of the executable part of every PL/SQL program. BEGIN tells Oracle that the following section contains operation commands, rather than declarations or exceptions. A BEGIN program section is always terminated eventually by an END statement, telling Oracle that there are no more executable statements in the current block.

Blocks can be nested up to a depth of 200 levels, using the BEGIN...END construct, so there may be many BEGINs in a PL/SQL program, each one operating, in more traditional programming terms, like a nested subroutine. Each nested block is known as a *'sub-block.'*

## EXCEPTION

This optional part of a PL/SQL block allows the designer to implement routines for handling 'exceptions'. An 'exception' can be roughly defined as *'a pre-defined or designer-specified occurrence during the operation of a PL/SQL block'.* Whenever the defined action occurs, a piece of code may be triggered into action. The executable statements that constitute this code are defined in the EXCEPTION section of the PL/SQL block. Each exception will be named, either by the designer or by Oracle. There are a range of pre-defined exceptions for which the designer can allow, or, alternatively, exceptions may be specially written to take account of actions that the designer wants to trigger for exception-handling code. *The EXCEPTION section is entirely OPTIONAL, and is not essential to PL/SQL code for it to operate satisfactorily.*

## END

All PL/SQL blocks, nested or not, must determine with an END statement, together with a semi-colon. END tells Oracle that there are no more executable statements in the current PL/SQL block. If this block is nested within another block, then control will be passed up to the block within which the sub-block is nested.

# Writing V3 Triggers using PL/SQL

Like Structured Query Language, Oracle will automatically recognize PL/SQL statements, such as DECLARE, when they are typed in a trigger. The following points outline rules and suggestions for entering PL/SQL in a trigger:

- Key words may not be abbreviated (the designer must always type 'BEGIN', never 'BE', for example).
- Key words must not be split (use whole words only).
- Spaces must be placed between key words on a line.
- All object names, such as variables and constants, must appear in full, and may not be split on a line.
- Generally, each statement must terminate with a semi-colon (;), but keywords such as DECLARE, BEGIN, EXCEPTION, etc. that are types of section or construct initiator, should not.
- When it is entered, SQL will take exactly the same form as it does in non-PL/SQL use, although for the sake of readability some commands can be stated on a single line.
- PL/SQL commands may be entered in upper-case or lower-case letters: there is no case-sensitivity.
- PL/SQL blocks may be nested up to 200 deep.
- It is good practice to indent nested sections of code, though this is not a syntactical requirement.
- Short blocks of PL/SQL entered normally into a trigger can legally be entered without including the BEGIN and END statements. These blocks are known as '*Anonymous Blocks*' in Forms 3. This facility is not available in PL/SQL batch file programming.

# Special symbols and characters in PL/SQL

PL/SQL uses a range of symbols, several of which are also quite usual in Structured Query Language. Table 1.1 shows common uses of ASCII or EBCDIC symbols.

**Table 1.1 PL/SQL symbols**

| Character | Function or use |
|---|---|
| $_#ABCDEFGHIJKLMNOPQRSTU VWXYabcdefghijklmnopqrstuvwxyz 0123456789 | Standard alphabetic and numeric characters for commands and object names. |
| ( ) | Parentheses for functions and numeric expressions. |
| + - * / < > = | Used for standard mathematical work. |
| , | Comma used as list item separator. |
| . | Period used as decimal; in object names; or as buffer code entry terminator when testing or writing using the SQL*Plus interpreter. |
| ' | Apostrophe for character delimits. |
| : & | Ampersand and colon used to indicate host variables (colon is the 'modern' version). |
| := | Used for variable assignment. |
| ** | Used for exponentiation (raising to powers using integers). |
| \|\| | Broken bar (often printed as twin vertical bars) used for string concatenation. |
| << >> | 'Wigwam' symbols used to delimit character labels. |

# Including comments in program code

**- - comment text.**
**/* comment text */**
**/* comment**
**text */**

PL/SQL provides two methods of placing textual program comments within the structure of a program. The first uses double hyphens to indicate that the rest of the line will be a comment. The second uses an 'open quote, close quote' construct where the 'quotes' are represented by a forward slash and an asterisk. The latter method allows comments to be split across two or more lines of the SQL Buffer, but not where there should be any operable program code. For example:

```
/* ------------------------------------------- *
 * This is an example of including commenting  *
 * text within a program.  Notice how there is *
 * only one set of 'closing quotes' characters *
 * but text on multiple lines...               *
 * ------------------------------------------- */
DECLARE
   SNUM     NUMBER(4) := 3788;
BEGIN
   DELETE FROM RECRUIT R -- delete person in SNUM.
   WHERE R.SNUM = SNUM;
END;                     -- end of program.
```

# Four types of variables

PL/SQL can make use of four different types of variable in SQL*Forms as follows.

## GLOBAL.variable

Datatype Assignment: Implicit

Datatypes: Character (effectively also Number, depending on context).

A GLOBAL variable is a SQL*Forms variable declared implicitly at some stage before it will be processed in a PL/SQL trigger (or, for that matter, a V2 trigger, where GLOBAL variables may be used just as they were in Forms 2.3 and earlier) or as part of the processing in the trigger. In V2 a value is placed into a GLOBAL variable using SELECT INTO or the Macro COPY. In V3 a value can be assigned with a simple assignment statement, or a PL/SQL SELECT INTO.

## SYSTEM.variable

Datatype Assignment: Implicit

Datatypes: Number (Read Only), Character (Read Only)

A SYSTEM variable is a SQL*Forms-maintained variable that contains information about the way Forms is running—for example, the current Field being processed and to which block it belongs. SYSTEM variables can be referenced in PL/SQL but may not be changed (one, SYSTEM.MESSAGE_LEVEL, may be changed, though). Table 1.2 on page 18 shows the names of SYSTEM variables.

## PL/SQL variable

Datatype Assignment: Explicit

Datatypes: Number, Character, Boolean, Date

A PL/SQL variable is one that is declared at the start of a piece of PL/SQL code in the DECLARE section of that code. It will exist for the runtime of the piece of code concerned and is not designed to last beyond this. Variables may be of several datatypes, and may be treated in various ways, discussed below.

## Local variables: Form fields

Datatype Assignment: Explicit

Datatypes: Number, Character, Alphabetic, Time, Date, Datetime, etc.

Form fields may be used as local variables. They may take an assignment in PL/SQL, or, using the more traditional V2 Triggers, from SQL in a trigger step. The datatype of the field will be defined by the designer when he or she creates it on-screen or within the Field Definition Spread Table or Form.

## Table 1.2 The names of SYSTEM variables

| System variable | Value |
|---|---|
| SYSTEM.TRIGGER_BLOCK | Current BLOCK being *processed.* If referenced in a KEY trigger, will contain the value of the position of the cursor before execution began. |
| SYSTEM.TRIGGER_RECORD | The sequence number of the current record being processed, in relation to all others held in the current block. |
| SYSTEM.TRIGGER_FIELD | Current ***BLOCK.field*** being *processed.* If referenced in a KEY type trigger, will contain the value of the last field before trigger execution. |
| SYSTEM.FORM_STATUS | Status of the Form in which the cursor sits. CHANGED (contains at least one changed record), NEW (contains only new records), QUERY (a query is open.) |
| SYSTEM.BLOCK_STATUS | Records the status of the block containing the cursor. It may be: CHANGED (block contains at least one changed record), NEW (contains new records), or QUERY (contains only valid records retrieved from the database.) |
| SYSTEM.RECORD_STATUS | Current record: CHANGED, INSERT (Changed Status, but record not in the database), NEW, QUERY (valid, and retrieved from the database.) |
| SYSTEM.CURSOR_BLOCK | Current BLOCK. |
| SYSTEM.CURSOR_RECORD | Current RECORD's sequence number. |
| SYSTEM.CURSOR_FIELD | Current ***BLOCK.field.*** |
| SYSTEM.CURSOR_VALUE | Actual value contained by the field containing the cursor. |
| SYSTEM.CURRENT_FORM | Name of the current FORM being run. |
| SYSTEM.LAST_QUERY | Contains the entire text of the SQL query last used to populate a block. |
| SYSTEM.LAST_RECORD | Contains the value **TRUE** (the current record IS the last sequential record in this block) or **FALSE** (it is not.) |
| SYSTEM.MESSAGE_LEVEL | Controls system error message severity levels. It may take the following values:<br>0 All levels.<br>5 Reaffirms an obvious condition.<br>10 Indicates operator made procedural error.<br>15 Declares operator attempted to make Form function in a manner for which it was not designed.<br>20 Declares operator cannot continue desired action due to trigger error or outstanding existing error.<br>25 Indicates condition that may result in incorrect functioning.<br>>25 Indicates message severity that cannot be suppressed using this system variable. |

# SQL*Forms V3 SYSTEM variables

SYSTEM.variablename

In addition to GLOBAL variables, SQL*Forms supports a series of variables that maintain system information. These may occasionally be of use to the system designer, and so a selection are referenced here. Just as GLOBAL variables are all prefixed with the word 'GLOBAL', so system variables are all prefixed by 'SYSTEM'. Their values should not be adjusted by the designer.

# Declaring PL/SQL identifiers: datatypes

```
DECLARE
    variable  datatype;
    variable  datatype := expression;
    variable  datatype NOT NULL := expression;
    constant  CONSTANT datatype := value;
    constant  CONSTANT datatype := expression;
```

PL/SQL allows the definition of variables and constants in a straightforward manner in the DECLARE section of the PL/SQL block. The variables and constants are, of course, simply spaces in memory that allow the temporary storage of data of a type specified, where the value may change during the course of the program run. Naturally, the language can also use GLOBAL and SYSTEM variables and fields that have already been created.

In PL/SQL, variables may be assigned a NOT NULL specification. This takes effect in the BEGIN part of the program, and prevents the assignment of a NULL value to the variable.

Constants are similar to variables in that they are spaces in memory where data can reside, but they will remain fixed throughout the running of the block, and will have a known value assigned to them at the start, in the DECLARE section, using the assignment operator, :=. Table 1.3 details the datatypes available. Rules are as follows:

- Each of the statements listed in the DECLARE section is terminated by a semi-colon.
- Variable names are not case-sensitive and may be up to 30 characters in length (A-Z, 0-9 and underscore, hash, and dollar are all permitted naming characters, and this is the standard Oracle Object-naming convention).
- By default, all variables are initialized to NULL. (Be wary, though, that this does actually mean 'NULL' as some mathematics can be disrupted if this fact is ignored!)
- Variables declared using an expression are initialized every time the PL/SQL block is entered.
- Expressions can contain references to previously defined variables or constants in the current DECLARE.

**Table 1.3 Declaring PL/SQL identifiers: datatypes table**

| Datatype or argument | Meaning |
|---|---|
| BOOLEAN | 'Boolean' variable: a tri-state variable definition, this datatype may store only the values TRUE, FALSE, or NULL. Values contained here cannot be inserted into a database column, nor can the PL/SQL SELECT or FETCH (see later) commands place values into a Boolean variable or constant. |
| CHAR(n) or VARCHAR2(n) | Character of length n up to 32 767 characters as from PL/SQL version 1.0.32; 255 from V1.0.00 through V1.0.31. (VARCHAR2 is for use with Oracle7 and PL/SQL Version 2: it retains old CHAR functionality when CHAR is upgraded for ANSI SQL compliance to pad with spaces to the width of the column or variable.) Note that this differs from the Database CHAR, which has a maximum length of 255 characters! |
| DATE | Date datatype taking a date value from 1 January 4712 BC to AD 31 December 4712. |
| NUMBER | Numeric of up to 38 digits. |
| NUMBER(x) | Numeric with length x up to 127 digits (up to 38 may be significant). |
| NUMBER(x, y) | Numeric with length x up to 38, and where y digits may form the decimal scale: the scale represents how rounding will occur, using the same arguments allowed in TRUNC( ) and ROUND( ) functions, from –87 to 127. A scale of 0 will round to an integer precision. |
| CONSTANT datatype | The named item is a constant, not a variable. |
| CONSTANT datatype := assnt | A constant taking the value produced by the expression in the <assnt> clause. This may be any valid PL/SQL expression (i.e. any standard Oracle SQL function, number, character, or date datum, or other acceptable evaluated assignment expression). |

- Forward references are *not* allowed: variables and constants must always be pre-defined, even where they will only contain a NULL value initially.
- Within the same PL/SQL block each variable or constant name must be unique but the names may be exactly the same in different blocks if desired.
- Fields may not be defined in the DECLARE section, though they may be referenced in PL/SQL code.

# –Example DECLARE section–

There may be any combination of different types of declaration in the DECLARE section. For example:

```
DECLARE
    SURNAME     CHAR(10);
    N1          NUMBER := 23.4567;
    JOINDATE    DATE;
    INCEP       DATE := '28-JAN-67';
    N2          NUMBER := SQRT(ROUND(N1 / 3.4, 2));
    MAXBONUS    NUMBER NOT NULL := 3000;
    RETIRE1     CONSTANT NUMBER(2) := 60;
    STOCKOUT    BOOLEAN := FALSE;
BEGIN
    ....
```

Note: Additional identifier %TYPE is discussed below. What happens with two separate but identically named variables in the same program is discussed later.

# -Declaring identifiers: %TYPE-

DECLARE
    *variable* [*owner.*]*table.col* %TYPE;
    *variable* [*owner.*]*table.col* %TYPE := *expression*;
    *constant* CONSTANT [*owner.*]*table.col* %TYPE;
    *constant* CONSTANT [*owner.*]*table.col* %TYPE := *expression*;

As part of the range of datatypes allowed in PL/SQL, Oracle have provided the %TYPE attribute. This enables a variable or constant to take on the same attributes as an equivalent database table's column, specified as part of the definition clause. The definition may include the full owner, object, and column name.

LONG datatype columns should not transfer data to a variable declared using %TYPE, nor should data be assigned to variables based upon LONG definitions. Using LONG, therefore, is not generally recommended. For example:

```
DECLARE
    PHONE      DCTDBA.CLIENT.PHONE%TYPE;
    SURNAME    RECRUIT.SURNAME%TYPE;
    BONUS      CONSTANT   RECRUIT.BONUS%TYPE := 1250;
BEGIN
    ....
```

# Moving data: SELECT...INTO

SELECT *standard_clause*$_1$,
*...,*
*standard_clause*$_n$
INTO block.field_*or_variable*$_1$,
*...,*
block.field_*or_variable*$_n$
FROM *[owner.]table_or_view*$_1$,
*...,*
*[owner.]table_or_view*$_n$
WHERE *condition*
*any other clauses...;*

The SELECT command is much the same in PL/SQL as it is in SQL elsewhere. That is, it operates normally except that there must be an INTO clause included in standard syntax in order to send data to the correct place in the program, record field, or variable.

By comparison with its normal usage, the SELECT command is not used as a standalone function in PL/SQL: it will almost always be employed in the context of placing a value into one or more variables or fields. It should be emphasized that variables must have been declared prior to use. The idea is that the programmer can then use the values of retrieved rows' data within the program for assignments, conditional branching, tests, re-insertion, or whatever.

The FROM clause will contain the name of a VIEW or TABLE from which the data will come—*never the name of a block!* It should be noted that

> In PL/SQL, SELECT can only ever return *one* row or set of values at a time.

In order to make PL/SQL process more than one line, therefore, looping and fetching commands must be used together with a pointer that will look at the *current* row in a referenced table. Such an operation must make use of a CURSOR, and this subject is dealt with elsewhere.

The following is a small sample program that outlines some of the major points in the use of SELECT... INTO in PL/SQL.

## Moving data: Mixed examples

```
DECLARE
    CURR_BONUS          NUMBER(9,2) := 0;
    BON_COPY            NUMBER(9,2) := 0;
BEGIN
    SELECT     R.BONUS * 1.15
    INTO       CURR_BONUS
    FROM       RECRUIT R
    WHERE      R.SNUM = 3107;
    BON_COPY   := CURR_BONUS;
    :b1.bonus := curr_bonus;
    :GLOBAL.surname := :b1.surname;
    :GLOBAL.syschecker := :SYSTEM.cursor_field;
    ...
END;
```

BON_COPY is used simply as an example of assigning a value using an assignment operator. Likewise, an imaginary :B1.BONUS field is assigned the content of CURR_BONUS, etc. The rules are as follows:

- Assignments may make use of any standard SQL functions or expressions (such as NVL( ), TO_CHAR( ), etc), and pseudo-columns SYSDATE and USER without a table reference.
- A SELECT statement in PL/SQL may only ever return one row or set of values at a time. An error (an 'exception' in PL/SQL) is raised if more than one row is returned, even though the SQL may be legal by itself.
- The FROM clause must always contain the name of the table or view from which data are coming. (Remember, too, that table access will always work faster than view access.)
- Standard SQL SELECT syntax, expressions, and operators are permitted and can be used normally.
- You should always prefix SQL*Forms Block and/or field names, GLOBAL, and SYSTEM variable names with a colon (:) where a reference is made to their value or content (either testing or setting).

## What happens when different Variable Objects have the same name?

Often in a program or a SQL*Forms application there may be one or more fields or variables that share the same name. In an ideal program this will never happen, but in the real world it can easily occur, due simply to the complexities of programming in a Fourth Generation Language. The following program illustrates the precedence that PL/SQL applies:

```
DECLARE
    BONUS       RECRUIT.BONUS%TYPE;
    CURSAL      RECRUIT.CURSAL%TYPE;
BEGIN
    /* ---first example---------------- */
    SELECT      BONUS,
                CURSAL
    INTO        BONUS,
```

```
                CURSAL
     FROM       RECRUIT
     WHERE      SNUM = 4009;
     /* ---second example-------------- */
     SELECT     BONUS,
                CURSAL
     INTO       :BONUS,
                :CURSAL
     FROM       RECRUIT
     WHERE      SNUM = 4009;
     /* ---third example--------------- */
     SELECT     BONUS,
                CURSAL
     INTO       :GLOBAL.BONUS,
                :GLOBAL.CURSAL
     FROM       RECRUIT
     WHERE      SNUM = 4009;
END;
```

There are four separate types of object in the example, each of which looks like the same thing:

```
BONUS              RECRUIT table column;
CURSAL             RECRUIT table column;
BONUS              PL/SQL variable (or field—see below);
CURSAL             PL/SQL variable (or field—see below);

BONUS              RECRUIT table column;
CURSAL             RECRUIT table column;
:BONUS             Block B1 screen field BONUS;
:CURSAL            Block B1 screen field CURSAL;

BONUS              RECRUIT table column;
CURSAL             RECRUIT table column;
:GLOBAL.BONUS      Global variable 'BONUS';
:GLOBAL.CURSAL     Global variable 'CURSAL'.
```

- In the first example Oracle knows that BONUS and CURSAL are PL/SQL variables because the INTO clause cannot be used to insert values into table rows, so it must be used here to place values into host variables (screen fields, GLOBAL variables in SQL*FORMS), or PL/SQL variables. The other two references, in the SELECT clause, can only be table columns from

RECRUIT because they have no colon prefix and PL/SQL assumes that this is a standard SQL query.

- In the next example, :BONUS and :CURSAL are parsed as HOST VARIABLES because PL/SQL treats colon-prefixed variables in this way. *A host variable in SQL*Forms must be a Screen Field if it is not a GLOBAL variable.* It is possible to reference a field in a Form simply by calling it in the format :FIELD, whatever its 'full' name really is, providing that the field's name is unique throughout the *whole Form.* It is not usually good practice to do this, though, for obvious reasons (confusing; not apparent where it belongs; not apparent what type of variable it is, etc.).
- In the final example, the :GLOBAL variables are obviously just that: they cannot be mistaken for columns or other types of variable.

# Entering a V3 Trigger in SQL*Forms V3

Unlike the requirements for entering a V2 Trigger in Forms, Version 3 Triggers are much simpler! First, log on to SQL*Forms using the appropriate password and user name:

1. Choose the Triggers Option from the Main Menu;
2. Press [insert record] when the Spread Table appears. (Note: if your trigger will be the first trigger in the screen then you will not need to press this.)
3. Enter the trigger name. There is a list of values available if you forget them all.
4. If this will be a block scope trigger only, then you need not enter any more details since the assumption will always be that this is a Block Scope trigger. If you would like to make it a field level trigger, simply type in the name of the field with which the code will be associated. If you would like the trigger to be associated with a block (or Block field) other than the one displayed, type over the displayed block.
5. Press [change display type], and complete any other details, then move to the scroll region in the centre of the screen in order to enter code. (There is no need to [zoom in] as there is with V2 trigger steps. Note: you can write *either* a V2 or a V3 Trigger for a named trigger, *not* both types in the same trigger!)

Figure 1.2 shows a graphic of the V3 Trigger Definition Spread Table and Fig. 1.3 a graphic of the V3 Trigger Definition Form.

```
Action  foRm  Block  Field  Trigger  Procedure  Image  Help  Options
                          Trigger Definition

   Trigger Name        Block Name          Field Name        Trigger   Show
                                                             Style     Keys
   key-commit          b1                  alpha             V3        [ X ]
   key-nxtfld          b1                  alpha             V3        [ X ]
   key-prvfld          b1                  alpha             V3        [ X ]

Enter the name of the trigger.
Frm: PLSQEX       Blk: b1        Fld: alpha       Trg: key-prvfld  <List><Rep>
```

Figure 1.2 V3 Trigger Definition Spread Table.

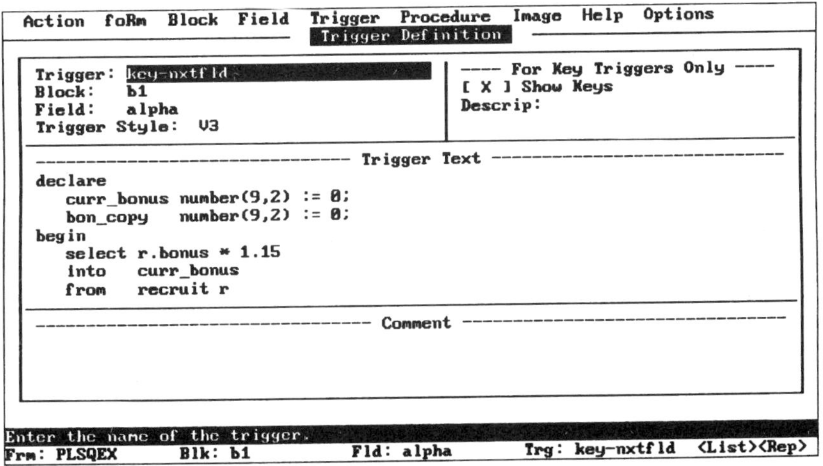

```
Action  foRm  Block  Field  Trigger  Procedure  Image  Help  Options
                          Trigger Definition

 Trigger: key-nxtfld                 ---- For Key Triggers Only ----
 Block:   b1                         [ X ] Show Keys
 Field:   alpha                      Descrip:
 Trigger Style: V3

 ------------------------------ Trigger Text ------------------------------
 declare
    curr_bonus number(9,2) := 0;
    bon_copy   number(9,2) := 0;
 begin
    select r.bonus * 1.15
    into   curr_bonus
    from   recruit r

 -------------------------------- Comment ---------------------------------

Enter the name of the trigger.
Frm: PLSQEX       Blk: b1        Fld: alpha       Trg: key-nxtfld  <List><Rep>
```

Figure 1.3 V3 Trigger Definition Form.

# Using the compiler and compilation errors form

If you are not familiar with compilers, this one may seem a little daunting. The idea of the compiler, of course, is that it takes any program code that you write, then parses it, converting it into machine code or a special code that is more easily readable by the software you use. All PL/SQL in Forms must be compiled before it can be included in a Generated Form.

The compiler can be daunting because it will not 'sit back' passively and let the designer store rubbish: it complains! (Though it may be switched off until Generation, if desired.) The SQL*Forms V3 compiler looks through all the code the designer writes, and checks it for (roughly) the following:

- Illegal constructs (types of complex or incorrect statement)
- Non-existent object references (fields, variables...)
- Semantic errors ('phraseology')
- Syntax errors ('typing')
- Anonymous Blocks: these will have a BEGIN and an END statement added to them automatically.

If errors are found, and you are generating the Form from the SQL*Forms environment, they will be written to a file called *formname.ERR*, otherwise, they

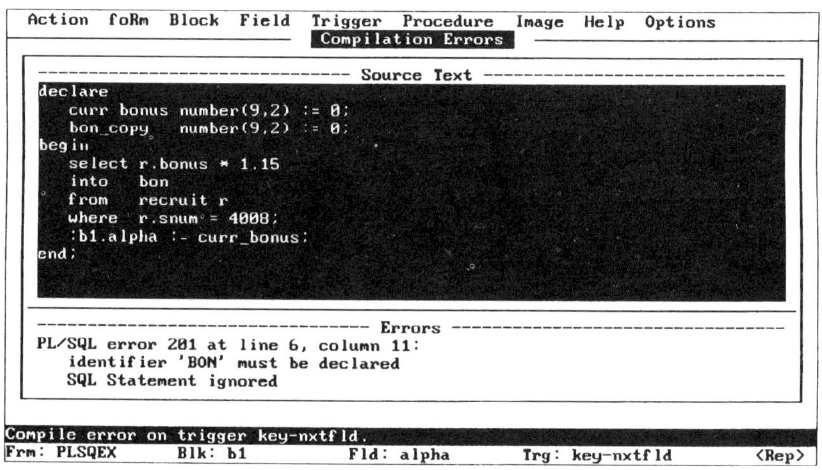


*Figure 1.4 The SQL*Forms Compilation Errors Form screen.*

will be flagged and displayed in the Compilation Errors Form shown in Fig. 1.4. The designer can scroll through the errors displayed by moving into the 'Errors' scroll region.

# Practical Session One

**Hint:** *It is suggested that the reader standardize on the operation 'SAVE' and 'GENERATE'. On many sites the 'SAVE' option has not been used for earlier versions of SQL*Forms, as these sites standardize on not storing applications in the database. As we shall see later, SAVEd Forms allow designers to access other Forms applications in order to COPY and REFERENCE stored procedures and other objects into current applications. This is a marked change from earlier implementations, and is related to the general changes in the Oracle7 DBMS release. Remember to use the SAVE option for your practical session examples, therefore, to avoid problems during the course of your study. You should ensure that you have created the example database for Parallel Universe Limited as detailed in Appendix A in order to test and debug your code.*

In this practical session make use of the PL/SQL commands and structures discussed only up to this point. Remember that because a command is included in a trigger this does not mean that it will actually run! It is up to you to see that there are appropriate command sequences to ensure this. Be careful about declarations and assignments: your referenced object must *exist* before you reference it! *Remember!* [accept] your trigger, once it is written. You must *generate* before you execute.

1 First, log in to SQL*Forms using the appropriate password and username assigned by your system operator or DBA. Create a New Form called PLSQEX. You will use this form for your initial PL/SQL practicals.
  Create a Control (NBT) Block called B1, and within it create the following fields: ALPHA *(width 20, Character)*, BETA *(width 40, Character)*, GAMMA *(width 40, Character)*, DELTA *(width 40, Character)*, EPSILON *(width 40, Character)*, none of which are Database Fields. In the following examples create the trigger code on the KEY-NXTFLD trigger of an appropriate field (ALPHA?), and then adjust the trigger or delete work when you have checked your answer.

2 Write a declaration section that performs the definitions shown in Table 1.4

**Table 1.4 Declaration section definitions for Exercise 2**

| Object | Datatype | Constant | Length | Null? | Assignment |
|---|---|---|---|---|---|
| surname | character | | 15 | Yes | ADYE |
| birthday | date | | | Yes | 18-NOV-62 |
| incep | date | | | No | 01-JAN-90 |
| retire_m | number | Yes | 2 | Yes | 65 |
| retire_f | number | Yes | 2 | Yes | 60 |
| joindate | date | | | Yes | 28-OCT-69 |
| cursal | *Exactly like CURSAL in table RECRUIT* | | | | 29400 |
| bonus | number | | 9, 2 | No | 825 |
| serve_length | number | | 9, 3 | Yes | round(months_between (incep, joindate), 3) |
| emp_flag | Boolean | | | Yes | TRUE |
| ret | date | | | Yes | |

**Hint:** *If you would like the compiler to test your work for you, create a three-line block that contains merely the keyword NULL, after your declarations. This does nothing at all, exactly like the NULL Macro in V2 code in SQL*Forms. Otherwise the compiler will complain that there is no code to run!*

3 Write appropriate code that will place ADYE's surname into the ALPHA screen field and his date of joining (JOINDATE) in the BETA field. Make sure that the joining displayed date appears in the same format as

Monday, 28th September, 1972.

4 Arrange for the GAMMA field to display the average salary of members of staff shown in the RECRUIT table, and for the DELTA field to show the average bonus received, by adjusting your program appropriately. The fields should display data in exactly the following way

```
Average Salary £nn,nnn.nn
Average Bonus £nn,nnn.nn
```

You *must not* use any Form Field *implicit* formatting for your answer. You should take account of any spaces between the figures and the sterling symbol. You might like to note, as an added challenge, that the sterling sign is illegal in conversion function pictures!

**Hint:** *you might find the Left-of-string-trimming LTRIM(x, y) function useful here, where x is the string, y, the character removed.*

5 By making use of the RETIRE_M variable, write code that will obtain the approximate date of Adye's retirement, based upon the total number of months between his birth and this time. The result will be placed in RET.

6 Finally, adjust your PL/SQL program (well, it is a program, now!) so that EPSILON will contain the details shown in Fig. 1.5. Note: the idea is to write the code that does this; do not type it in by hand—that's cheating!

**Hint:** *Adye will retire upon the final day of the month of his last year with his present company. You might find that your implementation of SQL*Forms objects to some of the date formatting commands working in a 'normal' way; if this is the case, try to get as close as you can to a correct answer. You will see in Fig. 1.5 that every attempt failed to make the code get rid of the space between the 'r' of 'October' and the comma! See if you can manage it.*

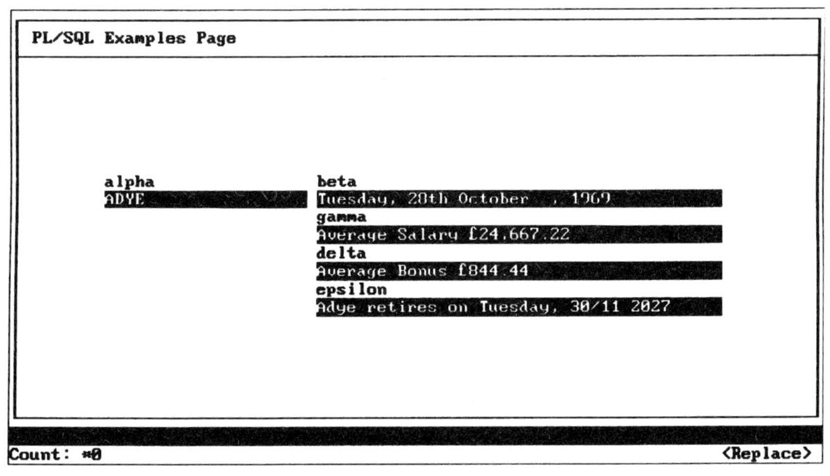


*Figure 1.5 Example screen display for Question 6.*

# CHAPTER TWO

# CURSORS

## CURSOR

```
DECLARE
   CURSOR cursorname
          IS select_clause;
   CURSOR cursorname (parameter parameter_datatype)
          IS select_clause;
```

In the previous chapter we saw that PL/SQL provides a whole range of processing options but that there was one overriding problem: *PL/SQL can only ever process one row of table data at a time* (except DML commands, which are covered in Appendix B). In order to process more than one row there would have to be multiple SELECT statements.

This makes the language very clumsy, because there must be vast amounts of program code written to achieve what would be very simple to do for single rows, or even 'by hand', re-entering data. There is one construct, however, that in combination with iterative and conditional controls transforms PL/SQL into a very powerful tool. This is the idea of the CURSOR.

> A CURSOR, in the context of PL/SQL, is most accurately thought of as a 'pointer' to a current row, or, alternatively, as a 'work area' in memory in which Oracle can maintain data about multiple-row retrievals.

A cursor is declared in the DECLARE section of the program. It may either be a straightforward, 'simple' cursor, declared using a SELECT statement, or it may take parameters and their datatypes also, *<parameter>* and *<parameter_datatype>* respectively, in the general form at the beginning of this chapter.

> A PARAMETER, in the context of Cursors, is like a type of local cursor variable that can take a new value each time the cursor is initialized.

Examples of cursor declaration are shown below.

## Simple cursors

(Note: usage is discussed later.)

### Example cursors

```
DECLARE
    CURSOR LOWERSAL
    IS SELECT     R.SURNAME,
                  R.CURSAL
       FROM       RECRUIT R
       WHERE      R.CURSAL <= 19300;
    CURSOR PERSON
    IS SELECT     R.*
       FROM       RECRUIT R;
BEGIN
    ...
```

### Rules for simple cursors

- Cursors must always be declared in the DECLARE section of the PL/SQL program code that will use them.
- The cursor's SELECT statement may not use the INTO clause.
- The SELECT statement may otherwise use any standard SQL clauses, functions, or constructs that are normally permitted, including subqueries, joins and relational algebra.
- A cursor is accessed (and can *only* be accessed) within the program by using OPEN and FETCH commands (see later in this chapter for details of these commands).
- A cursor may return zero, one, or many rows, and each of these states can be processed.
- A cursor's name may be up to 30 characters in length.
- The word 'SQL' cannot be used as a cursor name.
- Cursors do not work like variables—they are quite distinct, and cannot be assigned values or be referenced in DML commands. They are certainly *not* used for placing values into tables!
- Host variables (:VARIABLE) may be used in the WHERE clause of the cursor's select, if desired.

## Parameterized cursors

(Note: usage is discussed later.)

### Example cursors

```
DECLARE
 CURSOR  VARI_SAL(SAL_MAX NUMBER, SAL_MIN NUMBER)
 IS     SELECT     R.SURNAME,
                   R.CURSAL
        FROM       RECRUIT  R
        WHERE      R.CURSAL BETWEEN SAL_MIN
        AND        SAL_MAX;
 CURSOR  OLDER_PEOPLE (BIRTH DATE)
 IS     SELECT     R.SURNAME,
                   R.SNUM
        FROM       RECRUIT R
        WHERE      R.BORN < BIRTH;
BEGIN
 ...
```

### Rules for parameterized cursors

- The cursor's parameter or parameters can *only* be used as inputs to the cursor with which they are associated. They can perform no other function in the program.
- Wherever parameters are declared for a cursor, that cursor *must* make use of them in its SELECT statement. *This is a requirement.* A cursor parameter may be employed wherever a constant can be used within a cursor's SELECT statement.
- A parameter's name may only be specified once. It may not be re-used within a declaration. Multiple parameters and their datatypes are separated by commas; the complete list of parameters, within brackets.
- A parameter may take one of only the following datatypes: BOOLEAN, CHAR, DATE, or NUMBER. A parameter's datatype may *never include a length specification.*
- Where a table's column has the same name as a cursor parameter, the COLUMN'S VALUE is assumed when the cursor is parsed. To ensure correctness, within the cursor's SELECT statement a parameter may be referenced in the form: cursorname.*parameter*
  For example, VARI_SAL.sal_max.

## OPEN

OPEN *cursorname*;
OPEN *cursorname*(*input_parameter*$_1$, ... , *input_parameter*$_n$);

OPEN is used to initialize a cursor defined in the previous section. The OPEN forces Oracle to evaluate the SQL associated with the cursor, and allocates resources for this operation. The results of the cursor's SELECT are placed in memory, and the cursor 'pointer' is set to a point just before the first retrieved output row.

> The complete set of rows retrieved by the cursor is known as the *'active set'*.

The <*cursorname*>, then, must be the name of a cursor that has been defined earlier in the program. The cursor referenced may or may not have one or more parameters. The following two examples show one cursor OPEN with and without parameters.

```
DECLARE
 CURSOR OLDER_PEOPLE(BIRTH  DATE)
 IS      SELECT       R.SURNAME,
                      R.SNUM
         FROM         RECRUIT R
         WHERE        R.BORN < BIRTH;
 CURSOR PERSON
 IS      SELECT       R.*
         FROM         RECRUIT R;
BEGIN
 OPEN PERSON;                      --opened without any parameters
 OPEN OLDER_PEOPLE('01-DEC-61'); --opened with BIRTH parameter
...
END;
```

- If parameters were defined in the CURSOR declaration, they must be present in the OPEN clause. There must be the same number of parameters as there were parameter declarations, and *they must appear in the same order* in which they were defined in the cursor declaration.
- Remember that the parameter's value is passed to the cursor's SQL for use there: data cannot be brought back to the program from the cursor's SQL code using parameters.
- Parameters *must* have the same datatype as the cursor expects: characters will not suddenly magically be accepted for input to a NUMBER datatype parameter, for example!

# —CLOSE—terminating use—

CLOSE *cursorname*;

Once a cursor is no longer required within a PL/SQL block it should be CLOSEd. The CLOSE command will re-assign the cursor memory space if appropriate. One CLOSE command should be issued for each OPEN cursor when it is no longer needed within the program. It is good practice always to close any remaining cursors in the last lines of a program. Thus,

```
DECLARE
     ...
     whatever
     ...
BEGIN
     OPEN  S_DET(AVAL, BVAL, GVAL, DVAL);
     OPEN  PERSON;
     OPEN  OLDER_PEOPLE('01-DEC-61');
     ...
     lines of program code
     ...
     CLOSE  OLDER_PEOPLE;
     CLOSE  PERSON;
     CLOSE  S_DET;
END;
```

- Once it has been CLOSEd a cursor cannot be used again, and will yield an error (PL/SQL 'exception') if any attempt is made to use it, unless OPEN is used, or a special type of looping construct makes use of it (a type of loop, the FOR Loop, with Implicit Cursors, is not considered in this book).
- A cursor can be re-opened by issuing the OPEN command again. This will re-evaluate any parameters declared for the cursor, and will re-initialize the active set.

# Designer's notebook: an aside about parsing cursors

The following notes relate to the manner in which cursors are evaluated, or parsed, by Oracle when it is processing programs written in PL/SQL.

1 'Explicit' cursors defined in the DECLARE section—there may also be 'implicit' cursors, but these are outside the scope of this book—are generally parsed by PL/SQL only the first time they are OPENed. Therefore, the associated SQL statement is also only parsed upon this first occasion.

2 Each parsed SQL statement is placed into a 'cache', an area in memory. The parsed SQL statements, therefore, need only to be re-parsed if they have been pushed out of the cache by incoming new SQL statements.
3 A cursor's memory area must be re-assigned by using the CLOSE command. However, unless Oracle has used the memory space for something else, the CLOSEd cursor and its parsing information may remain there. Thus, if the programmer specifies that the old cursor is OPENed again within a program the associated SELECT statement need not be re-parsed.
4 If a cursor is CLOSEd then immediately re-OPENed, it will not require re-parsing.
5 Wherever a cursor does not require its SQL to be re-parsed it will obviously enable the associated program to run faster than if it had to be re-parsed, because Oracle will not have to expend any operational resources upon parsing it again.

# FETCH...INTO

FETCH *cursorname* INTO $variable_1$, ... , $variable_n$;

Once a cursor has been initialized, and has returned an active set, the FETCH command will take the first row from the set and pass the field data into variables; then the next row of the active set, and so on incrementally each time the command is parsed.

> All the variables used must have been defined earlier in the DECLARE section of the program, or they must be pre-defined block fields.

FETCH...INTO works in much the same way as SELECT...INTO, except for the fact that expressions are *not* allowed in the FETCH clause: it simply moves data.

At this point it should be stated that FETCH...INTO is virtually useless without a looping construct of some sort, and this is discussed below.

## Rules

- Any variables listed in the INTO clause must be stated in the same order, and have the same datatype, as the cursor SELECT from which their data will be coming. A field used must accept input and be of appropriate datatype.
- No expressions or functions may be included in the FETCH clause, ONLY the name of the cursor from which the data will be coming.
- A variable or list of variables (or fields) should be placed in the INTO clause. (Note: there is an advanced form of FETCH that will place results into a multi-field PL/SQL 'record'. This usage is outside the scope of this book.)
- Any variables in the WHERE clause of the cursor's SELECT are evaluated only when the cursor is first OPENed.
- *Only one row of data* will be retrieved by a FETCH.
- A FETCH may either be run multiple times or multiple FETCH statements may fetch data into multiple variables (see below).

# Multiple FETCHES without loops

The following program makes use of three variables that have been defined, SURN, CURS, and BORN, based upon columns in RECRUIT, and six GLOBAL variables. Naturally, in a real program, rather more would probably be written—but this is only an example.

Each of the FETCHes will transfer details from the next row of the active set, starting with the first, and working 'down' the set. It is, perhaps, easiest to think of the active set as being rather like a table, or view.

```
DECLARE
    CURSOR  F1
    IS  SELECT R.SURNAME,
               R.CURSAL,
               R.BORN
        FROM   RECRUIT R;
    SURN     RECRUIT.SURNAME%TYPE;
    CURS     RECRUIT.CURSAL%TYPE;
    BORN     RECRUIT.BORN%TYPE;
```

```
BEGIN
    OPEN F1;
    FETCH  F1  INTO
    :GLOBAL.SUR1, :GLOBAL.CUR1, :GLOBAL.BORN1;
    FETCH  F1  INTO
    :GLOBAL.SUR2, :GLOBAL.CUR2, :GLOBAL.BORN2;
    FETCH  F1  INTO
     :GLOBAL.SUR3, :GLOBAL.CUR3, :GLOBAL.BORN3;
    FETCH  F1  INTO
     SURN, CURS, BORN;
    CLOSE F1;
END;
```

# Cursors and explicit cursor attributes

| | | |
|---|---|---|
| **Explicit**: | *cursorname*%NOTFOUND | |
| | *cursorname*%FOUND | |
| | *cursorname*%ISOPEN | |
| | *cursorname*%ROWCOUNT | |
| **Implicit**: | SQL%NOTFOUND | |
| | SQL%FOUND | |
| | SQL%ISOPEN | (*always FALSE!*) |
| | SQL%ROWCOUNT | |

Each cursor opened in memory has four attributes, %NOTFOUND, %FOUND, %ISOPEN, and %ROWCOUNT. The attributes can be used rather like variables, and checked for values or states. This information can be used to control program flow, and its most obvious application is in the use of looping constructs, time-saving tests or value transfers.

%NOTFOUND, %FOUND, %ISOPEN are 'Boolean' attributes because they may only take the values 'FALSE' (traditionally, 0) or 'TRUE' (traditionally, 1). They can also be NULL, but that does not really count as a value! The last attribute, %ROWCOUNT, will contain a decimal integer (whole number) and is rather like an ordinary variable in this respect.

## Explicit cursors: cursorname%attribute

Whenever a cursor is executed, it will return zero, one, or many rows that will make up the active set. The %FOUND and %NOTFOUND attributes relate to this. (We shall discuss the values that these attributes may take, and under what circumstances, in a page or so!) They may be referenced either as SQL%FOUND, SQL%NOTFOUND, in which case they will always relate to the most recently OPENed cursor; or, rather more safely in logical terms, as *cursorname*%FOUND and *cursorname*%NOTFOUND, where their relationship is explicitly stated. Likewise, %ISOPEN and %ROWCOUNT.

*Cursorname*%ISOPEN will always be set according to whether or not the named cursor is OPEN. *Cursorname*%ROWCOUNT will yield the number of rows retrieved or affected by the contents of the cursor (the memory work area—also known as a 'context area'.) Therefore %ROWCOUNT effectively shows the number of the 'current row' in the active set relative to the first row when used with an incremental FETCH operation.

# Cursors and implicit cursor attributes

| | | |
|---|---|---|
| **Implicit**: | SQL%NOTFOUND | |
| | SQL%FOUND | |
| | SQL%ISOPEN | (*always FALSE!*) |
| | SQL%ROWCOUNT | |

The cursor attributes can also relate to DML statements (INSERT, UPDATE, DELETE and SELECT), and will indicate whether or not an action has occurred. Here, an IMPLICIT CURSOR is opened for use with the DML statement by Oracle itself. As with any normal SQL statement, a cursor will be implicitly opened for a SQL statement contained in a PL/SQL Block.

Obviously, here implicit cursor attributes can *only* take the form SQL%*attribute_name,* since no explicit cursor can be associated with a DML statement. An implicit cursor's attributes will indicate whether or not the associated DML statement actually affected any rows in the database.

*SQL%ROWCOUNT* will show how many rows were affected by the SQL in the cursor. *SQL%ISOPEN* will always be FALSE for Implicit Cursors because they will be CLOSEd automatically upon completion of the DML instruction contained within them.

## Attribute action/contents table

Table 2.1 shows the status of each of the cursor attributes for a given occurrence. %ISOPEN will always be FALSE. Obviously, the table can be used to gauge the content of the cursor attributes where an Explicit Cursor is named. Remember that cursorname%ISOPEN will only evaluate to TRUE if the cursor tested in still OPEN. (Note: the topic of PL/SQL and DML commands is covered in Appendix B.)

**Table 2.1 Content of cursor attributes for given actions**

| **Action** | **SQL%FOUND** | **%NOTFOUND** | **%ROWCOUNT** |
|---|---|---|---|
| *INSERT 1 or > 1 rows* | TRUE | FALSE | 1 or n |
| *UPDATE 1 or > 1 rows* | TRUE | FALSE | 1 or n |
| *DELETE 1 or > 1 rows* | TRUE | FALSE | 1 or n |
| **SELECT 1 row* | TRUE | FALSE | 1 |
| **SELECT > 1 row* | TRUE | FALSE | 2 |
| *INSERT 0 rows* | FALSE | TRUE | 0 |
| *UPDATE 0 rows* | FALSE | TRUE | 0 |
| *DELETE 0 rows* | FALSE | TRUE | 0 |
| **SELECT 0 rows* | FALSE | TRUE | 0 |
| *FETCH with 0 rows left* in the active set... | FALSE | TRUE | 0 |
| *FETCH 1 row* | TRUE | FALSE | 1 |
| **SELECT INTO with 0 rows returned...* | FALSE | TRUE | 0 |
| **SELECT INTO with > 1 row returned...* | TRUE | FALSE | 2 |

* It is important to remember that a SELECT used outside the context of an explicit cursor must never return more than one row. If it does, PL/SQL cannot process the information and will yield an error. The '2' value is produced regardless of the number of rows actually returned by the offending statement, and is designed to be trapped using a designer-defined exception routine, if desired.

# Iteration: simple or 'infinite' LOOPs and EXIT

```
LOOP
    ...
    EXIT WHEN condition;
    ...
END LOOP;
```

Loops, or iterative structures, are a useful and indeed essential part of any Third Generation Language. They are included in PL/SQL principally in order to allow for the repetition of parts of the program code, thus saving re-statement (re-coding) and consequent parsing overheads. A looping construct is especially useful with cursors because it will allow the same FETCH statement to be executed repetitively, using the same local or global variables.

With simple loops using the LOOP...END LOOP construct some form of exit statement must be completed in order for the looping operation to terminate at some point. This is provided with the EXIT WHEN statement, included within the body of the loop code. Conditional control using the IF statement can also be included, and this is covered later in this chapter.

A simple loop example is:

```
...
BEGIN
    OPEN PERSON;
    LOOP        —notice no semi-colon here!
        FETCH PERSON INTO PERS, SAL, BON;
        EXIT WHEN PERSON%NOTFOUND;
        ...
        program code
        ...
    END LOOP;
    CLOSE PERSON;
END;
```

- A basic loop must include an EXIT, GOTO, or RAISE (for exceptions) statement in order to terminate it. The loop construct always has the statement END LOOP as its last clause.

- Loops may be nested, but there is no clear definition of the maximum nesting depth.
- The EXIT clause, used to terminate a loop, will usually be of the form shown above. The EXIT will test the currently open cursor to discern whether or not there are any more records in the active set. The test construct is an attribute of the cursor, and has already been discussed in this book. For alternative constructs, see below.

## Looking more closely at EXIT WHEN

```
...
EXIT WHEN condition;
...
```

EXIT WHEN can, in fact, take any condition that is suitable. It operates rather like the IF..THEN construct that we shall meet shortly. *<condition>* may be any acceptable conditional test supported within PL/SQL, and may use any legal combination of the following elements:

| | |
|---|---|
| Logicals: | AND OR NOT |
| Expressions: | IS [NOT] NULL |
| | [NOT] BETWEEN *a* AND *b* |
| | [NOT] LIKE *a* |
| | [NOT] IN (*list_or_expression*) |
| Cursor Attributes #1: | cursorname*%NOTFOUND* |
| | cursorname*%FOUND* |
| | cursorname*%ISOPEN* |
| | cursorname*%ROWCOUNT* |
| Cursor Attributes #2: | *SQL%NOTFOUND* |
| | *SQL%FOUND* |
| | *SQL%ISOPEN* |
| | *SQL%ROWCOUNT* |
| Comparisons: | < > <= >= = <> != |
| Arithmetic Ops: | + - * / ( ) |
| Functions: | *Any legal SQL function of the type f(x).* |

# –Iteration: simple FOR loops–

**FOR *index_variable* IN *start_exp .. end_exp* LOOP**
**END LOOP [*label_name*];**
FOR *index_variable* IN REVERSE *start_exp .. end_exp* LOOP
END LOOP [*label_name*];

The FOR Loop construct is an almost traditional Third Generation Language construct. It differs from simple loops by allowing a variable, or <*index_variable*> to be used as a step counter, counting upwards or downwards (using the <REVERSE> clause) until a known end-point. The starting and ending integers are defined by the two parameters, <*start_exp*> and <*end_exp*> in the general form above.

The following example shows a simple loop stepping upwards from 1 to 30:

```
FOR CNTR IN 1..30 LOOP
        FETCH whatever...;  —example command only
        ...
END LOOP;
```

The implementation of FOR also allows named loops, by including the label within 'wigwam' symbols, << and >>. Names are always placed on a single, otherwise empty, line, just above the object to which they relate. For example:

```
<<firstloop>>
FOR COUNTR IN 1..20 LOOP
      ...
      <<secondloop>>
      FOR COUNTR IN 1..5 LOOP
            ...
      END LOOP SECONDLOOP;
      ...
END LOOP FIRSTLOOP;
```

Here

- COUNTR in <<firstloop>> could be referred to in <<secondloop>> as FIRSTLOOP.COUNTR.

- Within <<secondloop>>, the <<secondloop>> index variable, also called COUNTR, could be referred to as SECONDLOOP.COUNTR to avoid confusion.

*If this syntax is not used, errors can arise,* since PL/SQL will assume that the locally named index variable is referenced. Notice, also, that it is possible to *include the name of the loop in the END LOOP* clause to enhance readability and simplify operation and debugging.

# —Iteration: FOR loop rules—

- The *<index_variable>* need not be declared: it is *implicitly declared* by its placement in the FOR statement, and will be of NUMBER datatype. It *cannot* be referenced outside the loop in which it was implicitly declared.
- An index variable will be treated as if it were a constant within the loop: its value will remain until the next iteration.
- A variable declared outside the loop and referenced within it *may not take the same name* as the *<index_variable>* for that loop unless a label is used to identify the index in the form

  LOOP_NAME.*variable_name*

- A variable of the same name as an index variable, referenced from a DECLARE section definition must be referenced using the same syntax, otherwise PL/SQL will assume that the local variable takes precedence. Thus,

```
<<volcano>>
DECLARE
    snowflake NUMBER;
    dogfish   NUMBER;
BEGIN
    ...
    FOR snowflake IN 1..25 LOOP
        ...
        volcano.snowflake := 23456 * dogfish;
        ...
    END LOOP;
    ...
END volcano;
```

> **Note:** the END statement for the BEGIN clause may also take a label: that used for this section of code, first referenced immediately prior to the DECLARE.

# Conditions: —IF...THEN...ELSIF...ELSE—

IF *condition* THEN *statement(s)*;
[ ELSIF *condition* THEN *statement(s)*; ]
[ ELSE *statement(s)*; ]
END IF;

The IF statement is one of the most fundamental programming constructs in computing. It is implemented in PL/SQL to provide a sophisticated state-testing operator, of the type that was previously only possible using the Success or Failure of a WHERE clause in a SELECT block in SQL, when programming in SQL*Forms trigger steps.

In the above text, the square brackets, [ and ], indicate optionality, the simplest form of this statement being IF..THEN..END IF. The separate clauses are defined below:

*IF* Tests a condition to see if it evaluates to a TRUE state.

*THEN* Executes the PL/SQL statement or following list of statements (separated by semi-colons) if the condition in IF was TRUE (was satisfied).

*ELSIF* (*Optional*) If the original IF condition evaluates as FALSE, this clause performs a test of the condition stated in the ELSIF clause (which will go on to perform a THEN statement).

*ELSE* (*Optional*) If program control has 'dropped through' the THEN and ELSIF clauses without firing their PL/SQL, execute the statement or statements included after the ELSE clause.

*END IF;* Terminates the IF clauses, warning the PL/SQL engine that there are no more tests in this series of clauses. Note the space between the two words!

# IF... conditional tests supported

In the above general form <*condition*> may be any acceptable conditional test supported within PL/SQL, and may use any legal combination of the following elements:

| | |
|---|---|
| *Logicals:* | AND OR NOT |
| *Expressions:* | IS [NOT] NULL |
| | [NOT] BETWEEN *a* AND *b* |
| | [NOT] LIKE *a* |
| | [NOT] IN (*list_or_expression*) |
| *Cursor Attributes #1:* | *cursorname*%NOTFOUND |
| | *cursorname*%FOUND |
| | *cursorname*%ISOPEN |
| | *cursorname*%ROWCOUNT |
| *Cursor Attributes #2:* | SQL%NOTFOUND |
| | SQL%FOUND |
| | SQL%ISOPEN |
| | SQL%ROWCOUNT |
| *Comparisons:* | < > <= >= = <> != |
| *Arithmetic Ops:* | + - * / ( ) |
| *Functions:* | *Any legal SQL function of the type f(x).* |

# Example IF...THEN...ELSIF...ELSE clauses

This shows how a grade statistics calculation program might operate for a course examination assessment. The variable GRADING has had a value entered into it in the earlier part of the program, and is being tested to ascertain into which band the examinee's result will fall. If it contains a NULL, then, obviously, running through the rest of the tests is pointless.

If something unusual has happened, and the result cannot be caught by the earlier ELSIFs, as the logic implies, then the last part of the code will ensure that the erroneous record is flagged and dealt with, presumably by another part of the code. *Indentation is wholly optional, but it makes writing and debugging code much easier.*

```
BEGIN
    ...
    other program code
    ...
    IF GRADING IS NULL THEN
        :GLOBAL.UNGRADED_NAME := SURNAME;
    ELSIF GRADING < 39.5 THEN
        FAILURES := FAILURES + 1;
    ELSIF GRADING >= 39.5 AND GRADING < 50 THEN
        THIRDS := THIRDS + 1;
    ELSIF GRADING >= 50 AND GRADING < 60 THEN
        LOWER_SECONDS := LOWER_SECONDS + 1;
    ELSIF GRADING >= 60 AND GRADING < 70 THEN
        UPPER_SECONDS := UPPER_SECONDS + 1;
    ELSIF GRADING >= 70 THEN
        FIRSTS := FIRSTS + 1;
    ELSE :GLOBAL.ERROR := RECORD_NUMBER;
        :GLOBAL.GRADE_ERR_NAME := SURNAME;
    END IF;
    ...
    other program code
    ...
END;
```

Other legal constructs include the following examples and similar constructs are quite legal, provided that there is always an END IF for each initial IF statement:

```
1. IF  condition1 THEN
        IF  condition2
        END IF;
   END IF;

2. IF  condition1  THEN action
        ELSIF  condition2  THEN
              IF  condition3
              END IF;
   END IF;
```

# Branching: GOTO and naming blocks

GOTO *label_name*;

GOTO will send program control to the point identified by the *<label_name>* argument in a PL/SQL program. The label must be a standard Oracle name, but it may be anything that the standard rule will allow. There are some particular restrictions on the use of GOTO, though, and these are listed below.

Usually, GOTO will not be used by itself, but will form part of the result of one or more conditional statements, such as IF...THEN; but the command can stand alone if need be. For example, the following construct is quite legal:

```
BEGIN
   ...
   GOTO volcano;
   ...
   <<volcano>>
   DECLARE
      snowflake  NUMBER;
      dogfish    NUMBER;
   BEGIN
      ...
   END;
   ...
END;
```

as is:

```
BEGIN
   ...
   IF B > 6 THEN GOTO brand_loyalty;
   ELSIF whatever...
   ...
END;
<<brand_loyalty>>
BEGIN
   ...
```

# —More rules about GOTO—

- GOTO may not be used to branch to an Exception Handler Section.
- GOTO may branch to another place within the current Block, or within an enclosing Block.
- From an Exception Handler section a GOTO may branch ‘out’ to an enclosing Block but not to the current Block for which this is the Exception Handler.
- Control cannot be transferred into the middle of a sequence of statements, such as LOOPs and IF clauses.
- GOTO must jump to a label just before an executable statement, BEGIN, or DECLARE. Statements such as END LOOP and END IF are *not* regarded as executable, they are statement terminators.

*It is a bad idea to over-use GOTO statements:* their use can make code complex and difficult to debug, and it is recommended that considerable care be taken before using more than one in a piece of program code! Wherever possible, the designer is urged to become used to the idea of employing other methods, such as Form-Level Procedures (discussed later in this book), before going ‘down the procedural path’. Removal of constructs such as GOTO will always increase robustness of code and enhance ease of maintenance by encouraging the ‘centralization’ of code modules. ‘Spaghetti code’ is a nightmare best left to older procedural languages.

# ——Labels in PL/SQL——

*<<label_name>>*

Labels are a useful inclusion in the PL/SQL language, and we should briefly summarize their rules here. There is no formal name in PL/SQL for the << and >> signs. It is suggested that they be known as ‘wigwam symbols’ in memory of the story that says the greater than and less than symbols in modern mathematics were based on native American art because the authors of the groundbreaking book, *Principia Mathematica* (1915) by Russell and Whitehead, had this interest.

- Labels must always be placed in ‘wigwam’ symbols, << and >>, when they are stated at a point in the run of code.

- Labels may be any text up to 30 characters in length, provided that the text does not conflict with standard Oracle naming conventions.
- If a label is used to identify a block it must also terminate the block:

```
<<label>>
BEGIN
    ...
    code;
    ...
END label;
```

- A label may also prefix any DECLARE section in a PL/SQL program.

# Practical Session Two

1 Write a PL/SQL trigger on KEY-COMMIT defined for the ALPHA field that will produce the following effect as closely as possible by summing only the first three salaries in the RECRUIT table. You should not make use of the FOR LOOP or SELECT INTO constructs in your answer, but you are expected to use a cursor.

> **Hint**: *Make sure that your loop is not infinite! Do not worry too much if the sum does not come out to be the same as this one*—provided it's correct!—*because Oracle will not necessarily always have the* same *first three rows: as you know, it decides for itself how it wants to store data and, especially if you have inserted additional rows into a table, there is a decreasing likelihood that the same three rows will remain as the first three rows throughout the life of the table, even though no rows are actually deleted from it. The first three salaries were originally those of Shackle, Gartner, and Raja, but the idea is not to reference surname values at all in your code. See Fig. 2.1 for an example of the screen graphic expected.*

2 For this question, type over (rename) the KEY-NXTFLD trigger you wrote for the previous question: call it OLD_NXTFLD (make sure you use an underscore, not a hyphen!). For this solution, we shall re-use KEY-NXTFLD for the ALPHA field, just to keep life simple.

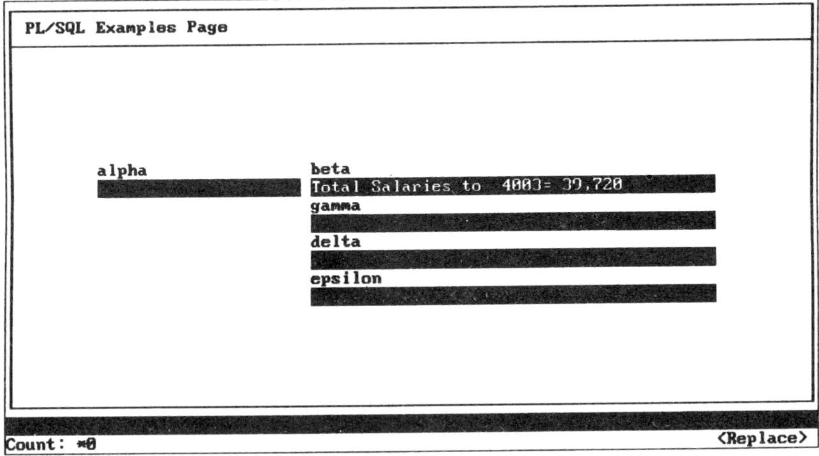


*Figure 2.1 Screen graphic for Question 1.*

Your aim is to write a short PL/SQL trigger program that will check through the CLIENT table, whenever fired, to determine the following:

1 How many non-British companies are stored?
2 How many companies are based in Inner or Greater London?
3 How many, if any, records are missing a value in the Country column?
4 How many, if any, records are missing a telephone number?

Figure 2.2 shows the expected output and output format.

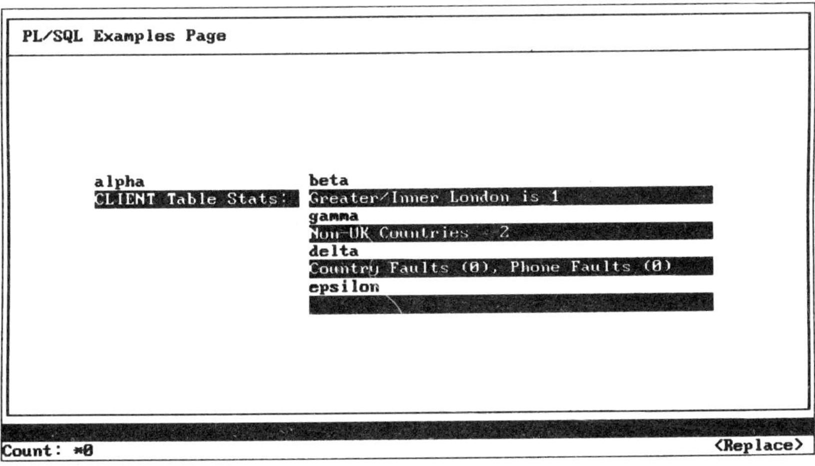


*Figure 2.2 Expected output and input format.*

**Hint:** *Because of the way the database has been set up, you may need to make a couple of assumptions, especially regarding Question (2) because the ADDRESS2 and ADDRESS3 columns are too indeterminate to help, probably through a designer error with which you must now cope. Try to write all your code in PL/SQL: do not be tempted to slip into SQL, though you* will *need it in a special PL/SQL construct: that's fine. You may find it easier to think in terms of Sections of Code in order to construct your program: a DECLARATION Section, a PROCESSING Section, an OUTPUT Section. Remember that output of numbers may need a conversion to Character datatype to avoid oddities and Compiler Errors.*

3 Create a KEY-CREREC (the [create record] key) trigger on the ALPHA field. It is not relevant operationally: it has been chosen just as a different trigger.

Your Managing Director is shortly having a meeting with a prestigious recruitment client, and needs to know various different statistics. Your Manager has suggested that you might like to write a piece of code that will answer one particular question immediately, but that can be re-used subsequently as a permanent programmed feature of the recruitment system.

So what does the MD want to know? Ah! The MD wants to know the *average (mean) number of different skills possessed by recruits presently stored in our database, to two decimal places.* The original designer of the recruitment database system has left you with a challenge that you must now solve. How will you determine how to differentiate between the different skills a person may have, given that there is no list of skills; that the skills can be virtually anything you can think of (so there is no list to check against); and that there may be different spellings; also, that there may be any number of skills, from none to n, per person? Output should appear as follows in Fig. 2.3, though you might get a different output figure: 5.33 was obtained only for the original nine rows and their skills.

**Hint:** *Well, this should be fun! Look carefully at the format of the skills stored in the SKILLCOM column in the RECRUIT table. It is very obvious, but so obvious you might not spot it. This is a genuinely 3GL solution to a problem posed by a bit of poor 4GL design.* Make sure *that your program can cope with the odd case of the person who has* no skills! *You are entitled to make the reasonable assumption that each skill has been entered with care.*

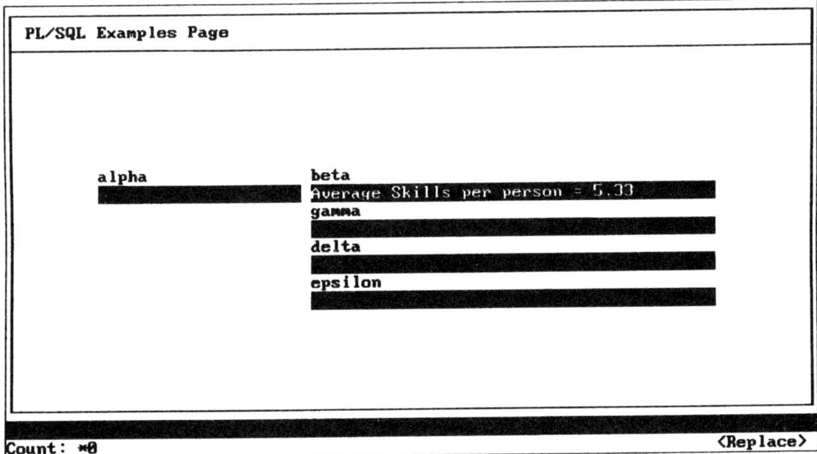


*Figure 2.3 Example screen display for Question 3.*

CHAPTER THREE

# EXCEPTIONS

## Introduction

```
DECLARE
        declarative statements...
BEGIN
        executable statements...
EXCEPTION
        exception handler statements...
END;
```

An 'EXCEPTION' Section is an optional part of a PL/SQL Block that allows the designer to implement routines for providing enhanced or special functionality when 'Exception' errors (or states) occur during runtime. An 'Exception' can be roughly defined as: 'a pre-defined PL/SQL or designer-specified occurrence during the operation of a PL/SQL Block.'

Whenever the defined action occurs, a piece of code may be triggered. The executable statements that constitute this code are defined in the EXCEPTION section of the PL/SQL block. Each Exception will be named, either by the designer or by Oracle ('Internal' or 'Pre-defined' Exceptions).

There are a range of pre-defined Exceptions for which the designer can allow, or, alternatively, 'User-Defined' Exceptions may be specially written to take account of actions that the designer wants to trigger Exception-handling code. As we saw earlier, and as experience now shows, the Exception Section is entirely optional, and is not essential to PL/SQL code for it to operate satisfactorily.

When an error or specific condition occurs, an Exception is 'RAISED': normal program execution determines and control is passed to Exception Handler code.

> Exceptions may be 'raised' internally by PL/SQL itself, or may be explicitly raised by the designer, using the keyword RAISE within a program. They exist to 'trap' a known or anticipated occurrence, and allow the program to deal with it.

In either instance, the effect will be to call a routine stored in the EXCEPTION section of the current PL/SQL Block. Exceptions may catch any type of activity desired, whether SUCCESS or FAILURE is the basis for them. Each of the elements in the construction of Exception Handling routines is discussed below.

## Declaring User-Defined Exceptions

```
DECLARE
exception_name1   EXCEPTION;
...
exception_namen   EXCEPTION;
other clauses...
```

User-Defined Exception Declarations can appear at any point in any legal DECLARE clause in a PL/SQL program. Exceptions may take any name desired by the designer, subject to Oracle standard naming conventions and a length of no more than 30 characters (including underscores, etc.)

'Pre-defined Exceptions' are Exceptions that are already available automatically, and a list of these is given shortly: they need no declaration. Examples of special User-Defined Exceptions might be:

```
DECLARE
    grade_too_low          EXCEPTION;
    illegal_identifier     EXCEPTION;
    recruit_age_error      EXCEPTION;
    invalid_format         EXCEPTION;
    not_furry_enough       EXCEPTION;
    duplicated_value       EXCEPTION;
    ...
```

## EXCEPTION section

...
EXCEPTION
    WHEN *exception_name* THEN *pl/sql_statement(s)*;
    WHEN *exception_name* OR *exception_name* ...
        THEN *pl/sql_statement(s);*
    WHEN OTHERS THEN *pl/sql_statement(s)*;
END;

The EXCEPTION section takes this general form, each of the named Exceptions being 'stepped through' by the parser when a call is made to an Exception handler named by <*exception_name*>, and the <*pl/sql_statement*> in the THEN clause evaluated. There may be as many statements following the THEN clause as necessary, each terminated with a semi-colon. The logical OR may be used within the WHEN clause if desired, in order to perform the same set of statements for either or one of several possible exceptions. WHEN OTHERS THEN will allow for any other type of Exception that has not been handled, executing the <*pl/sql_statement(s)*> stated after the clause.

> The optional WHEN OTHERS Exception should always be the last Exception Handler in the EXCEPTION section.

It is important to realize that when an Exception Handler has completed its operation the current PL/SQL block will have been terminated, and control will pass back to whatever called the block in the first place: an 'outer' block, or whatever trigger or call initiated the running of the PL/SQL code in this block.

Obvious as it may seem at this point, it should be remembered that the function of Exception Handlers is to handle Exceptions! The designer should not treat them like subroutines in more traditional languages.

In SQL*Forms there will usually be a series of statements that make use of the pre-defined 'Packaged Procedures' supplied with the product, or call 'Form-Level Procedures' defined by the designer. Both these techniques are covered in the following chapter.

# User-Defined EXCEPTION examples

For example,

```
...
EXCEPTION
when grade_too_low then
     :b6.reporter := '*value error 1*';
when value_overflow then
     total_salary := total_salary / 10000;
     ov_flag := 1;
when illegal_user
or   unidentified_user then
     :GLOBAL.disable_delete := 'Y';
     :GLOBAL.disable_update := 'Y';
     if use_date = NULL then
        use_date := sysdate;
     end if;
     if auto_log = 'Y' then
        user_log := user;
     end if;
when OTHERS then
     ROLLBACK;
END;
```

As with other layout suggestions, the indentation is entirely optional and has no bearing whatsoever on the way the code is parsed: it will make life *much* easier when debugging or simply reading the code. Note that the END statement here will be the same as the END statement that determines the whole of the current PL/SQL Block, since the EXCEPTION section comes right at the end of the code.

## Triggering User-Defined Exceptions: RAISE

RAISE *exception_name*;

This command brings to life the Exception Handler named in the argument. Usually, RAISE is used as part of a conditional test, to determine the situation under which the Exception should be raised. For example:

```
...
IF EXAM1 + EXAM2 < 33.5 THEN
   RAISE grade_too_low;
ELSIF EXAM3 + EXAM4 < 44.5 THEN
   RAISE higher_grade_too_low;
END IF;
...
```

Control will jump to the Exception Handlers named in the two clauses as appropriate.

## Exception rules

- There may be any number of Exception Handlers defined: as many as the designer feels necessary.
- The same Exception name cannot be used twice in the same Block.
- Exceptions cannot be assigned values or used in Structured Query Language statements: they are *not* 'Objects' in the same way as fields and variables.

- Only local and global variables may be referenced in a Handler, not variables from Blocks within other PL/SQL programs or SQL*Forms applications.
- An Exception in an Outer Block cannot refer to an Exception within an inner Block.
- It is a bad idea to declare Exceptions that have the same names as existing Pre-defined Exceptions, because PL/SQL will override the Pre-defined Exception and this may conflict with standard code elsewhere in an Organization or Application suite.
- An Exception declared in a Sub-Block will override an Exception of the same name in an outer Block in the current PL/SQL program.
- Once an Exception Handler has completed its operation, the current Block will have been terminated or completed. It is illegal to go back into the Block from a statement in the EXCEPTION section. The whole Block must be re-run from the start.
- If no Handler is incorporated for a given Exception, the Exception will 'propagate' out to the enclosing Block, then out to the Block enclosing that one, and so on until a suitable handler is found, or a system Error message will be raised if there is no Handler at all, unless the OTHERS clause is used at some point.
- An Exception raised within an EXCEPTION section will propagate automatically outwards to the enclosing block if there is one or raise an error condition if there is not.
- It is illegal to use GOTO to jump to an Exception Handler, or out of an Exception Handler into its associated Block. It *is legal* to use GOTO to jump out of the current Block into a (non-Exception Handling!) part of an enclosing block.

Table 3.1 shows the list of pre-defined Exceptions for PL/SQL. *Note:* this table can only represent a very brief overview of these Exceptions. The interested reader is referred to *Oracle PL/SQL User's Guide and Reference Version 1.0,* April 1989 (revised November 1990), Oracle part No. 800-V1.0, Chapter 6, for full information.

**Table 3.1 Pre-defined Exceptions for PL/SQL**

| Exception | Explanation |
|---|---|
| zero_divide | An attempt has been made to divide a number by zero (the result is infinite, of course!). |
| value_error | An Arithmetic, Conversion, Constraint, Numeric, or String error has occurred other than that raising an INVALID_NUMBER Exception. |
| too_many_rows | A SELECT has returned more than ONE row. |
| timeout_on_resource | Timeout has occurred when Oracle is waiting for a resource. Usually an indication of abnormal Oracle instance termination. |
| storage_error | PL/SQL has run out of memory, or memory has been corrupted in some way. |
| program_error | PL/SQL has an indefinite internal system problem. |
| others | All other Exceptions not explicitly named. |
| not_logged_on | PL/SQL has issued a call to Oracle but has become disconnected from an instance or has not somehow logged on. |
| no_data_found | A single-row SELECT has returned no rows. Note that Group Functions such as AVG( ) always return a value, even if NULL, so this Exception would not be raised in this case. |
| login_denied | An invalid username/password was used at logon (SQL*Forms, SQL*Plus, ...). |
| invalid_number | Raised when attempted conversion of a CHAR string to a NUMBER fails because the characters do not represent a valid number. |
| invalid_cursor | An invalid or currently non-existent cursor is referenced (e.g. CLOSE for an already CLOSEd cursor). |
| dup_val_on_index | An INSERT or UPDATE has attempted to create two rows with duplicate values in a column with an UNIQUE index attached to it. |
| cursor_already_open | Attempt to open an already OPENed cursor. |

## The FORM_TRIGGER_FAILURE Exception

FORM_TRIGGER_FAILURE

In addition to the standard range of Exceptions available for use in PL/SQL, Oracle have provided another pre-defined exception that is specific to SQL*Forms Triggers, FORM_TRIGGER_FAILURE. A Version 3 Trigger, since it is entirely different in structure and operation to a V2 Trigger, will not normally fail, not least because there is no need to direct the logical flow of control using the concept of Success and Failure in the same way as earlier versions of the product allowed. However, there will be occasions when the designer wishes to force a trigger to fail explicitly and the FORM_TRIGGER_FAILURE exception has been designed to allow this. Upon FORM_TRIGGER_FAILURE being raised:

> SQL*Forms halts execution of the trigger and performs any appropriate post-failure processing.

For example, suppose that we wish to prevent a non-authorized user from entering a Form Application. If Failure is encountered during the execution of a PRE-FORM trigger, control returns to the Operating System or calling process, so Failure will prevent the current user from accessing the application. USER is the system variable, SQL.USER, of course, though it loses the 'SQL.' prefix in PL/SQL usage:

```
Trigger:    PRE-FORM
Style:      V3
begin
   if USER <> 'SDERIDOES' then
       raise form_trigger_failure;
   end if;
end;
```

# PART TWO

# Form-Level and Packaged Procedures, Packaged Functions

*Truly there is no end to this wondrous science; and when the sceptic sneers, 'With all these methods one ought to be able to make everything out of nothing,' the Qabalist smiles back with the sublime retort, 'With these methods One did make everything out of nothing.'*

***From 'Gematria', published in*** 777 and Other Qabalistic Writings of Aleister Crowley

*Aleister Crowley*

CHAPTER FOUR

# FORM-LEVEL PROCEDURES

## Introduction

This chapter begins by looking at Form-Level Procedures. These are the natural successors to User-Defined Triggers (now called 'User-Named Triggers') in earlier versions of SQL*Forms, and allow a designer to build up a library of personally authored or other routines that may be utilized in more than one application or application-suite for performing common functions.

The chapter continues by discussing the 'Packaged Procedures' and 'Packaged Functions' available with SQL*Forms Version 3. Many of the Packaged Procedures are exactly the same as the V2 macro language. Some Packaged Procedures even have the same names, but they are substantially enhanced by the addition of more sophisticated functions and facilities.

Packaged Functions are really all related to the types of operation that take place in the life of a running Form. They return information about the Forms environment as it operates, and the data returned can be used to direct program flow and alter the operation of a Form in a more advanced method than was previously possible. Both Packaged Procedures and Packaged Functions easily combine with the functionality afforded by PL/SQL, producing a powerful tool for SQL*Forms programming.

# Procedure definition

Form-Level Procedures have a special fill-in form associated with them that may be called up during design and implementation, by calling up the facility from the Main Menu directly. PROCEDURE DEFINITION is called whenever it is necessary to adjust or define a procedure created by the application builder.

There are two forms that the PROCEDURE DEFINITION screen may take, in common with other elements in the Form:

- *Procedure Definition Form* Shows details for one procedure only, on a complete screen.
- *Procedure Definition Spread Table* Shows details of one procedure in relation to all others in the current form.

The two versions of the screen are shown in Figs 4.1 and 4.2. The [change display type] function key is used to swap between them.

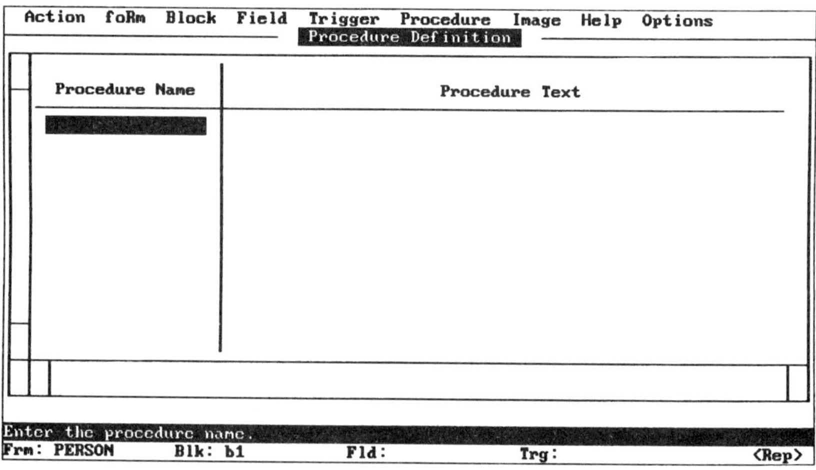


*Figure 4.1 Procedure Definition Spread Table.*

```
Action  foRm  Block  Field  Trigger  Procedure  Image  Help  Options
                            Procedure Definition

  Procedure Name:
  ----------------------------- Procedure text -----------------------------

Enter the procedure name.
Frm: PERSON       Blk: b1          Fld:           Trg:                <Rep>
```

*Figure 4.2 Procedure Definition Form.*

## Simple Form-Level Procedures

PROCEDURE *procedure_name* IS
    *any_local_pl/sql_variables_declared_here;*
BEGIN
    :
    *pl/sql_statements;*
    :
    EXCEPTION *optional_exception_handlers*;
END;

'Form-Level Procedures' are programs written in PL/SQL that belong to the Form itself, rather than to any lower-level object. They differ from straightforward trigger code because they are never associated with a time-related event in the same way as a trigger. That is, a Form-Level Procedure is an independent object within a Form. It must always take a certain structure, in common with any programming language, but it can be activated from any point in a Form at which a trigger may operate. The Procedure is invoked merely by stating its name within a PL/SQL trigger in the Form. It may even take parameters that can be passed to the Procedure code upon invocation (see later). In practice, a Form-Level Procedure looks more like some form of function itself, than a series of commands!

*Names for procedures must adhere to the standard conventions in Oracle*, that is, they may be any character string up to 30 characters in length, containing letters A to Z, numbers 0 to 9, and underscores, hashes or dollar symbols. Each name must start with a letter.

If the designer wishes to declare local PL/SQL variables, these can be declared immediately after the PROCEDURE name statement. Note that:

> Local variable definition in a Procedure does not require the use of the DECLARE keyword at the start of the Procedure.

Procedures have a major advantage in that they allow the designer to centralize code that will be common to many routines within the Form, or, as we have said, throughout an application suite (later notes explain this idea).

For example, the following procedure gives the person whose SALARY is contained in :GLOBAL.SALARY a pay increase of *n* per cent, where *n* is a decimal fraction contained in the global variable :GLOBAL.PERCENT.

```
PROCEDURE INCREASE_SALARY_PERC IS
BEGIN
   :GLOBAL.salary := :GLOBAL.salary *
      (1 + :GLOBAL.percent);
END;
```

Note that, rather oddly, the name of the procedure must be typed into the *Procedure Name* field on screen, as well as being listed within the procedure itself.

In a trigger elsewhere in the current Form, the INCREASE_SALARY_PERC procedure code may be invoked as follows:

```
BEGIN
    :
    :
    pl/sql_statements;
    :
```

```
    INCREASE_SALARY_PERC;
     :
     pl/sql_statements;
     :
     :
END;
```

Alternatively, if the designer wishes only this statement to be run, rather than a whole series of other commands and functions, they need merely enter the name of the procedure on a line by itself, as though it were a packaged procedure, in an anonymous block:

```
INCREASE_SALARY_PERC;
```

# Simple Form-Level Procedures: examples

Some people have difficulty in understanding how to use Form-Level Procedures for simple activities, especially if they have been used to Trigger programming and are not yet quite familiar with PL/SQL. The following examples show how some simple actions might be programmed using Form-Level Procedures. Remember that each Procedure may be called from any anonymous or 'traditional' PL/SQL block in a Form, but *only* from a V3-Style trigger.

### Example 1: Setting a field in a block called B10 and a GLOBAL variable

```
PROCEDURE set_tot IS
BEGIN
 :B10.totals := (:B8.total * 8) + :B7.total +
        :B3.total + 10000;
 :GLOBAL.set_flag := 1;
END;
```

**Example 2: Setting up and using two example local variables**

```
PROCEDURE analyse_detail IS
STAT_TOT          RECRUIT.CURSAL%TYPE := 0;
ALPHA             NUMBER := 10;
BEGIN
   /* ...too long-winded for real life! */
   STAT_TOT := :GLOBAL.TOT1 * ALPHA;
   STAT_TOT := STAT_TOT + 23.45;
END;
```

**Example 3: Running ANALYSE_DETAIL and SET_TOT procedures consecutively in a straightforward V3 Trigger**

```
BEGIN
   analyse_detail;
   set_tot;
END;
```

## Form-Level Procedures with parameters

PROCEDURE *procedure_name*
(*argument*$_1$ *type*$_1$ *datatype*$_1$, ... , *argument*$_n$ *type*$_n$ *datatype*$_n$)
IS
  *any_local_pl/sql_variables_declared_here;*
BEGIN
  :
  *pl/sql_statements;*
  :
  EXCEPTION *optional_exception_handlers;*
END;

Procedures may also take a parameterized form. Parameterized procedures have the major advantage that they can be made universal; that is, the procedure may take data from any variable that appears in the argument list at the point it is invoked. Parameters may be designated as 'IN' or 'OUT', for INPUT and OUTPUT.

An 'IN' parameter will take a value into the body of the procedure for use there; an 'OUT' parameter will be used for taking the result of the work performed within the procedure. This result can then be used in the code that called the procedure. By default, if not stated explicitly, a status of 'IN OUT' is set, allowing either direction.

| | |
|---|---|
| *<argument>* | is the name of the parameter, up to 30 characters. |
| *<type>* | is the definition of the usage of the argument:<br>*IN* Data flowing into procedure through this parameter.<br>*OUT* Data flowing out of procedure into variable placed here.<br>*IN OUT* No pre-defined direction. The *default* setting. |
| *<datatype>* | is the datatype of the parameter argument:<br>BOOLEAN *Binary True/False*<br>CHAR *Character (like PL/SQL)*<br>NUMBER *Numeric (like PL/SQL)*<br>DATE Date *(like PL/SQL)* |

# Parameterized procedure: example

As an example, suppose that we wanted to *universalize* the preceding procedure example:

```
PROCEDURE INCREASE_SALARY_PERC IS
BEGIN
   :GLOBAL.salary := :GLOBAL.salary * (1 + :GLOBAL.percent);
END;
```

We still want to achieve the same effect, but this time we do not want to pre-define the names of the variables that will be referenced in the Procedure itself. *We want to be able to use any variable we like at any point in the form.* Therefore let there be three parameters as follows (call them anything):

| | |
|---|---|
| ALEF | NUMBER for input, |
| BA | NUMBER for input, |
| JEEM | NUMBER for output. |

These will take the place of the pre-defined GLOBAL variables referenced in the preceding code, so they become

```
(alef in number, ba in number, jeem out number)
```

Hence, the suggested code in Fig. 4.3.

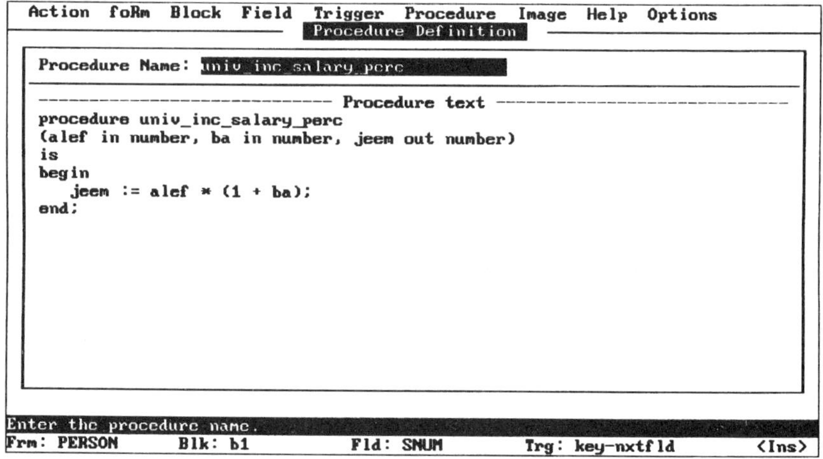

```
Action  foRm  Block  Field  Trigger  Procedure  Image  Help  Options
                          Procedure Definition

Procedure Name: univ_inc_salary_perc

----------------------------- Procedure text -----------------------------
procedure univ_inc_salary_perc
(alef in number, ba in number, jeem out number)
is
begin
   jeem := alef * (1 + ba);
end;

Enter the procedure name.
Frm: PERSON       Blk: b1          Fld: SNUM          Trg: key-nxtfld        <Ins>
```

*Figure 4.3 Example of a completed Form-Level Procedure.*

The Form-Level Procedure can be invoked very simply, thus. Suppose we have a simple KEY-NXTFLD trigger that contains the following text:

```
DECLARE
   ALPHA    NUMBER(3)   :=  0;
   SAL      NUMBER(3)   :=  100;
BEGIN
   UNIV_INC_SALARY_PERC(SAL,  .50,  ALPHA);
   :B1.RESULT  :=  ALPHA;
END;
```

Therefore,

`:B1.RESULT` will contain...?

# Practical Session Three

This practical session begins with the creation of a new Form, PERSON, then allows you to set up some Form-Level Procedures for it. This Form is the basis for further practical work. There are no trick elements in Question 1.

1 ***Important! Read all of this question first!***
For this first part of the practical, if you are not already, log on to SQL*Forms. Create a new Form with the name 'PERSON'. Create a default Block. Call it 'B1' or think of a suitable name for yourself. The block should have one row, and be based upon the table called RECRUIT in the Parallel Universe database.

Now, move into the Field Definition Screens and make the following settings. Note that the '-' implies the default setting should remain for this field. *You should leave the field sequencing until after redesigning the screen (the next part of this question).*

| *Field Name* | *Seq #* | *FLen* | *QLen* | *DLen* | *Attributes & Settings* |
|---|---|---|---|---|---|
| *Adjust the following:* | | | | | |
| SNUM | 1 | 6 | 6 | 6 | ON: Primary Key, OFF: Required |
| SURNAME | 2 | - | - | - | OFF: Required |
| FORENAME | 3 | - | - | - | ON: Uppercase |
| SEX | 4 | 3 | 3 | 3 | ON: Uppercase |
| BORN | 5 | - | - | - | Format Mask: DD-MON-YY |
| CURSAL | 6 | 11 | 11 | 11 | Format Mask: "£"99,999 |
| BONUS | 7 | 11 | 11 | 11 | Format Mask: "£"99,999 |
| SKILLCOM | 8 | 255 | 255 | 58 | Field Editor: (18, 15) |
| PACKAGE | 9 | 255 | 255 | 58 | Field Editor: (18, 15) |
| INCEP | 10 | - | - | - | Format Mask: DD-MON-YY |
| COMMENTS | 11 | 240 | null | 58 | Field Editor: (18, 15) |
| *Create the following:* | | | | | |
| *AGE* | *12* | *3* | *null* | *3* | *OFF: Input, Update, Query, Base Table* |
| *Datatype: NUMBER* | | | | | *ON: Echo, Displayed* |
| *NEXT_BIRTHDAY* | *13* | *24* | *null* | *24* | *OFF: Input, Update, Query, Base Table* |
| *Datatype: CHAR* | | | | | *ON: Echo, Displayed* |
| *TODAY* | *14* | *24* | *null* | *24* | *OFF: Input, Update, Query, Base Table* |
| *Datatype: CHAR* | | | | | *ON: Echo, Displayed* |
| *TOTREMU* | *15* | *11* | *null* | *11* | *OFF: Input, Update, Query, Base Table* |
| *Datatype: NUMBER* | | | | | *ON: Echo, Displayed*<br>*Format Mask: "£"999,990* |

*Make sure that you have GENERATEd and SAVEd by now!*

Now adjust the screen to resemble Fig. 4.4. Remember to check that the field sequences are as shown in the above table.

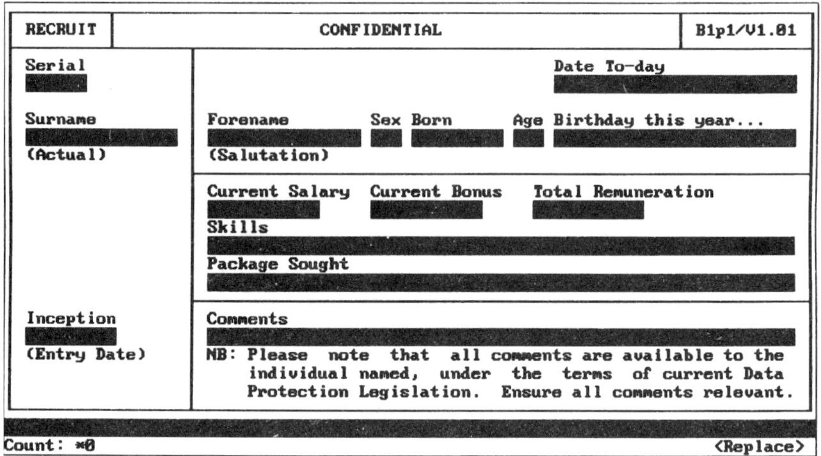


*Figure 4.4 Screen graphic for Question 1.*

2 Create a simple Form-Level Procedure that will place today's date into the :B1.TODAY field. Call it 'FILL_TODAY'. Remember, the idea is to do it programmatically: do not use field formatting! Output should appear something like, '`Tuesday, 17th Nov 1992`'.

*Do not create a trigger to fire your code yet, that comes in Question 5.*

*(Note: If you would like to test out your code, you can either create it first in a trigger, such as KEY-NXTFLD, then copy it to your Procedure using the editing tools (Cut, Copy, Paste) in the trigger editor, or you can create it entirely in a Procedure, then invoke it from a trigger of your choice.)*

3 Create another Form-Level Procedure. Call it 'FILL_REMU'. It will add together BONUS and CURSAL to yield a total remuneration figure in B1.TOTREMU.

*Do not create a trigger to fire your code yet, that comes in Question 5. Do not forget to SAVE if you have not already!*

4 Write a Form-Level Procedure that will place the current person's age in the AGE field, and that will display the day and date of their *birthday this current*

*year*, placing the result in the NEXT_BIRTHDAY field, such as '`Friday, 28th Aug 1992`'. Call your Procedure, 'FILL_BIRTHDAY'.

The idea is that the recruitment consultants can offer a more personal service to potential clients by sending them a card on their birthday, or mentioning it in conversation. You might like to look at the proposed layout graphic in Fig. 4.5 to see how the output for one recruit appears. *It is a little trickier to achieve this than you think at first, unless you have already thought through everything at once!*

*Do not create a trigger to fire your code yet, that comes in Question 5.*

5 Finally, create a PRE-RECORD trigger in Block B1 that will fire the three Form-Level Procedures you have created in practicals (2) – (4). Make sure you have DELETED any trial triggers you created for firing your Procedure code in the interim. *Do not forget to SAVE if you have not already!* Your final result at runtime will look something like Fig. 4.5.

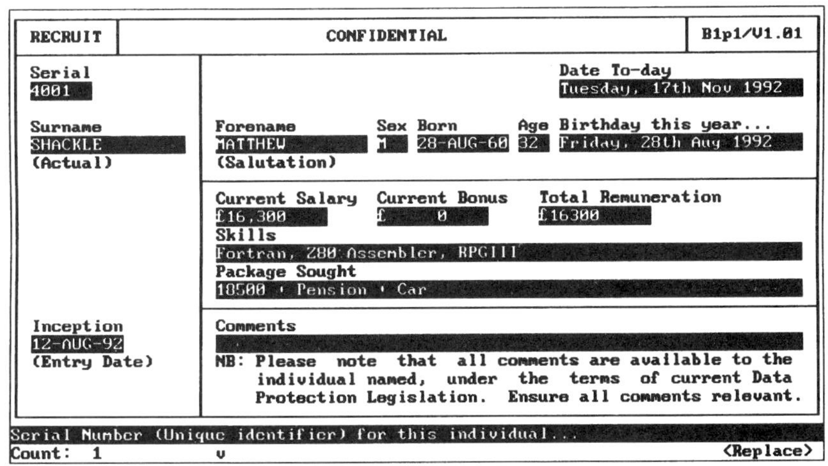


*Figure 4.5 Screen graphic for Question 4.*

# CHAPTER FIVE

# PACKAGED PROCEDURES

## Packaged Procedures introduced

*PACKAGED_PROCEDURE;*
*PACKAGED_PROCEDURE(arguments);*

Packaged Procedures are PL/SQL procedure names, very similar to Version Two Macros, but available for use in any Version Three trigger, or in legal PL/SQL anywhere in a Form. As with earlier versions of SQL*Forms macros, many of the Packaged Procedures map closely to function keys that are normally used by the Operator in order to control the way a Form works at runtime.

The names of all Packaged Procedures are pre-defined. The closest that the designer can get to writing new Packaged Procedures is to write Form-Level Procedures which (as we have seen earlier in this section) when entered in PL/SQL can appear exactly like Packaged Procedures and can be used in the same manner.

This chapter contains overview details of Packaged Procedures available with Forms 3 as standard. It looks principally at Non-Key Packaged Procedures, except where a key-type Packaged Procedure has additional functionality or arguments.

The idea of using Packaged Procedures is to perform the following tasks:

- Modify the default processing used by SQL*Forms for specific applications or to provide additional or altered functionality.
- Reduce or simplify complex or tedious data entry tasks.
- Control the manner in which an operator uses Forms by ensuring that their use of an application takes place in a pre-determined way, for example to ensure exact correspondence with a business function or equivalent real-world operation.

## A reminder about object referencing

SQL*Forms expects that objects referenced within PL/SQL are correctly identified. In Packaged Procedures this leads to some rather odd-looking, but quite logical, constructs. The golden rule is as follows:

> The names of objects other than PL/SQL variables should be referenced in single quotes.

Thus, we might have a series of Packaged Procedures (they are fairly obvious, even before we have looked at their functionality!):

```
CALL('stock_updater_form');
GO_BLOCK('person');
GO_FIELD('person.surname');
```

and references,

```
'SYSTEM.cursor_field'
'global.mannerism'
```

But declared PL/SQL variables would not appear in quotes:

```
PAY_INC := XCURSAL + ROUND(XBONUS * .125, 0);
```

# Trigger types and restrictions table

Table 5.1 shows pre-defined trigger names and the objects to which they most closely relate. The 'Imp levs' column shows within what scope a trigger may be used, and 'Commands allowed' indicates the types of code that are allowed within each type of trigger.

**Table 5.1 Pre-defined trigger names**

| Trigger type ('traditional' association) | BM | Trigger name | Imp levs | Commands allowed |
|---|---|---|---|---|
| FORM-Related | | Pre-Form | F | S U |
| | | Post-Form | F | S U |
| | | Pre-Commit | F | S U D |
| | | Post-Commit | F | S U D |
| | | On-Error | F B | S U |
| | | On-Message | F B | S U |
| BLOCK-Related | No | Pre-Block | F B | S U |
| | | On-Clear-Block | F B L | S U |
| | No | Post-Block | F B | S U |
| | | Pre-Query | F B | S U |
| FIELD-Related | No | Pre-Field | F B L | S U |
| | No | On-New-Field-Instance | F B L | S U R |
| | No | Post-Change | F B L | S U |
| | | On-Validate-Field | F B L | S U |
| | No | Post-Field | F B L | S U |
| RECORD-Related | No | Pre-Record | F B | S U |
| | | On-New-Record | F B L | S U |
| | | On-Validate-Record | F B | S U |
| | | On-Remove-Record | F B L | S U |
| | | On-Lock | F B | S U |
| | No | Post-Record | F B | S U |
| | | Pre-Update | F B | S U D |
| | | On-Update | F B | S U D |
| | | Post-Update | F B | S U D |
| | | Pre-Insert | F B | S U D |
| | | On-Insert | F B | S U D |
| | | Post-Insert | F B | S U D |
| | | Pre-Delete | F B | S U D |
| | | On-Delete | F B | S U D |
| | | Post-Delete | F B | S U D |
| | | On-Database-Record | F B L | S U |
| | | Post-Query | F B | S U |

**Table 5.1 Pre-defined trigger names (continued)**

| Trigger type ('traditional' association) | BM | Trigger name | Imp levs | Commands allowed |
|---|---|---|---|---|
| KEY Triggers | | Various... | F B L | S U R |
| USER-NAMED | | Any name chosen | F B L | S U R D (As calling Trigger) |

*Key:* F = Form, B = Block, L = Field, S = SQL SELECT Commands can be used.
U = Unrestricted Packaged Procedures can be used.
D = DML Commands can be used (INSERT, UPDATE, DELETE.)
R = *Restricted* Packaged Procedures can be used.
No = Not recommended where running on Block Mode equipment.

The following notes relate to Table 5.1.

## The BM column

This column indicates Triggers that are not recommended for use with Block Mode hardware. Block Mode equipment works by sending 'chunks' or 'blocks' of data to the computer's CPU, terminated by function key presses. This means that where an action, rather than a function key press, causes movement between, say, one field and another, the code related to a trigger defined within the FIELD scope cannot be fired until a function key is pressed to tell the CPU that the cursor has physically moved. On Bit-mapped and Character Mode systems, the CPU is aware at every moment where the cursor is, so it can easily process the appropriate level triggers.

## Precedence

The same name may be used for a trigger defined at different 'levels' within a Form. The concept of levels conflicts slightly with the more modern concept of Objects but it is still correct. The highest level is FORM, then BLOCK, then the lowest, FIELD. In order to deal with the fact that separate Triggers may have been implemented with the same name, SQL*Forms operates a *'Precedence'* mechanism such that the following rule applies:

> *Any Trigger implemented at Field Level will take precedence over a trigger of the same name implemented at Block Level, which will take precedence over a Trigger of the same name implemented at Form Level. Hence,*

> Field takes precedence over Block takes precedence over Form Level Triggers.

## U-TYPE: *Unrestricted* Packaged Procedures

An Unrestricted Packaged Procedure is a piece of coding in a SQL*Form that *will not interfere* with the basic functionality (or 'standard behaviours') of SQL*Forms when it is running an application. *These are permitted wherever the letter U is shown.*

## R-TYPE: *Restricted* Packaged Procedures

A Restricted Packaged Procedure is a piece of coding in a SQL*Form that *will affect or adjust* the basic functionality (or 'standard behaviours') of SQL*Forms when it is running an application. *Accordingly, these are not permitted except where indicated in the table with the letter R.*

## User-named triggers

These are triggers that take a name defined by the systems designer. They must always be called from a trigger that has a permitted name. The types of code permitted will be the same as those types of code permitted for the trigger in which the calling code is located. In SQL*Forms Version 3 they take an increasingly unimportant role because of the enhancement of Form-Level Procedures supported by this release of the product.

# Packaged Procedures' —restrictions and overview—

Like Macros, Packaged Procedures can have Restrictions on their use. Table 5.2 shows a list of the Restrictions (Rstn) that apply to non-Key Packaged Procedures in Forms 3. Key-related Packaged Procedures, together with their relationship to V2 Macros, are shown in Table 5.3 on page 84.

The 'Opt Args' column indicates whether the Procedure may have an argument; 'Rqd Args' indicates that the procedure must have an argument. 'U' indicates an Unrestricted Packaged Procedure; 'R' indicates a Restricted Packaged Procedure.

## Table 5.2 Restrictions

| **Packaged Procedure name** | **Opt. Args** | **Rqd Args** | **Rstn** |
|---|---|---|---|
| anchor_view | | • | U |
| bell | | | U |
| break | | | U |
| call | | • | U |
| call_query | | • | U |
| clear_block | • | | R |
| clear_eol | | | R |
| clear_form | • | | R |
| commit_form | | | R |
| copy | | • | U |
| copy_region | | | R |
| cut_region | | | R |
| default_value | | • | U |
| display_field | | • | U |
| display_page | | • | U |
| do_key | | • | R |
| edit_field | • | | R |
| enter_query | • | | R |
| erase | | • | U |
| execute_query | • | | R |
| execute_trigger | | • | U/R† |
| exit_form | • | | R |
| go_block | | • | R |
| go_field | | • | R |
| go_record | | • | R |
| hide_menu* | | | U |
| hide_page | | • | U |
| host | | • | U |
| list_values | • | | R |
| lock_record | | | U |
| message | | • | U |
| move_view | | • | U |
| new_form | | • | R |
| paste_region | | | R |
| pause | | | U |
| post | | | R |
| replace_menu* | | • | U |
| resize_view | | • | U |
| set_field | | • | U |
| set_input_focus* | | • | U |
| show_menu* | | | U |
| show_page | | • | U |
| synchronize | | | U |
| user_exit | | • | U |

See page 84 for notes on Table 5.2.

*These Packaged Procedures relate to the operation of the SQL*Menu product, and are outside the scope of this book but are shown here for completeness. Full details are contained in the *Oracle SQL*Forms Designer's Reference Version 3.0*, Oracle Part No. 3304-V3.0 0191, and in SQL*Menu documentation, to which the reader is referred.

†Depends upon the Restriction code applying to the commands used in the executed trigger. The command itself appears to take on Unrestricted or Restricted functionality depending upon usage.

Some Packaged Procedures, such as DEFAULT_VALUE, are included solely for downwards-compatibility, and are not necessarily recommended for use with SQL*Forms Version 3.0. Although use of these macros is not detrimental to application operation, if there is a more completely Version-3.0 orientated method, this would be preferable to ensure full upwards compatibility.

# Key-related Packaged Procedures' restrictions and overview

Table 5.3 shows Version 2 Macros, the equivalent Function Key presses, and the Version 3 Packaged Procedure name that is the equivalent. The former is included for completeness and is not covered in this book. The RSTN column shows the type of restriction that applies to this function: R implies 'Restricted'; U implies 'Unrestricted'. The Restrictions are defined in relation to the types of triggers in which these functions may appear within a SQL*Form.

**Table 5.3 V3 Packaged Procedures and V2 Macros and Restrictions**

| V2 Macro | Key function performed | V3 Packaged Procedure equivalent | Rstn |
|---|---|---|---|
| ABTQRY | [abort query] | abort_query | U |
| CLRBLK | [clear block] | clear_block | R |
| CLRFLD | [clear field] | clear_field | R |
| CLRFRM | [clear form] | clear_form | R |
| CLRREC | [clear record] | clear_record | R |
| COMMIT | [commit] | commit | R |
| CQUERY | [count query hits] | count_query | R |
| CREREC | [insert record] | create_record | R |

**Table 5.3 V3 Packaged Procedures and V2 Macros and Restrictions (continued)**

| V2 Macro | Key function performed | V3 Packaged Procedure equivalent | Rstn |
|---|---|---|---|
| DELREC | [delete record] | delete_record | R |
| DERROR | [display error] | display_error | U |
| DKEYS | [display keys] | show_keys | U |
| DOWN | [down] | down | R |
| DUPFLD | [duplicate field] | duplicate_field | R |
| DUPREC | [duplicate record] | duplicate_record | R |
| ENTQRY | [enter query] | enter_query | R |
| EXEQRY | [execute query] | execute_query | R |
| EXIT | [exit/cancel] | exit_form | R |
| HELP | [help] | help | U |
| LISTVAL | [list field values] | list_values | R |
| MENU | [menu] | block_menu | R |
| NXTBLK | [next block] | next_block | R |
| NXTFLD | [next field] | next_field | R |
| NXTKEY | [next primary key field] | next_key | R |
| NXTREC | [next record] | next_record | R |
| NXTSET | [next set of records] | next_set | R |
| PRINT | [print] | print | U |
| PRVBLK | [previous block] | previous_block | R |
| PRVFLD | [previous field] | previous_field | R |
| PRVREC | [previous record] | previous_record | R |
| REDISP | [refresh] | redisplay | U |
| SCRDOWN | [scroll down] | scroll_down | R |
| SCRUP | [scroll up] | scroll_up | R |
| UP | [up] | up | R |
| UPDREC | n/a | lock_record | U |

# —EXECUTE_TRIGGER( )—

EXECUTE_TRIGGER('*triggername*');

This Packaged Procedure is the direct equivalent of the older #EXEMACRO EXETRG *triggername* used in earlier versions of SQL*Forms, and is principally included for upwards-compatibility. It will call and execute the trigger named in <*triggername*>, usually a User-Defined one. With the introduction of PL/SQL and Form-Level Procedures, EXECUTE_TRIGGER should eventually become redundant, since Form-Level Procedures offer a far more sophisticated mechanism, not least because they may take arguments.

# –CALL( ), CALL_QUERY( )–

CALL('*formname*');
CALL_QUERY('*formname*');
CALL('*formname*', *hide_stat*, *rep_stat*);
CALL_QUERY('*formname*', *hide_stat*, *rep_stat*);

CALL will make control jump to the <*formname*> specified in the argument. The function will keep the calling Form active while the called Form is being processed, but then control will return to the calling Form at the end of processing, rather like a subroutine. If Oracle is unable to complete the call, then the cursor (NU) will return to the point in the calling Form from which it came. For example

```
CALL('contextual_help_7a', NO_HIDE);
```

CALL_QUERY will make control jump in a similar fashion, but the called Form will be in Query Mode only, that is, the operator can only perform SELECT type queries, and other DML commands will be illegal (INSERT, UPDATE, DELETE) in either triggered code or through ordinary Forms operation.

For both these packaged procedures, an internal SAVEPOINT is issued for the called Form. Should the CLEAR_FORM Packaged Procedure or function key cause a Rollback to occur, it will be back to this savepoint that the transaction will be rolled. *Note:* it is not clear from Oracle literature what the *name* of this savepoint will be, so it is suggested that if designers wish to make use of this facility in a structured way, they create a savepoint with an explicit name themselves and build in Rollback functionality, unless the automatic default operation will suffice for their application.

<*hide_stat*> may be:

*HIDE* Forces Oracle to clear the screen before drawing the first element of the called Form.

*NO_HIDE* Prevents Oracle from redrawing the screen, therefore if the first page of the called Form is smaller than the page that was last displayed, or in a different position to a small original page, then the new page will be displayed on top of the old page, or both smaller-than-screen-size pages will be displayed at once.

<*rep_stat*> may be:

*NO_REPLACE* If the Form has been used in conjunction with the SQL*Menu product, this parameter will ensure that the application will retain the current default Menu of the calling Form as the Menu with which it will be associated, otherwise the default Menu of the called Form will become the Menu used by the operator.

*DO_REPLACE* Forces any default Menu application set up with the called Form to become the default for the operator and for the session until control jumps back or elsewhere.

# NEW_FORM( )

NEW_FORM('*formname*');

This is similar to the CALL( ) Packaged Procedure, but this procedure will call a Form as though it were a wholly new Form. The calling Form will be terminated, and control will pass wholly on into the new Form, rather like starting a wholly new and separate program. For example:

```
NEW_FORM('stock_control');
```

The new Form will be run with the same runtime options as the Form that called it.

If the NEW_FORM Form was called from a Form that was itself called from a Form, then this first Form will be retained as a calling Form, and control will be passed back to it when the current Form terminates.

# EXIT_FORM( )

EXIT_FORM;
EXIT_FORM(*argument*);

This Packaged Procedure causes the termination of the current Form's operation: the NU is set to 'Outside Form'. If the current Form has been CALLed from another Form, then control will return to the calling Form. By default, SQL*Forms will prompt the operator to COMMIT any changes by displaying the appropriate Alert Box.

If an argument is used with EXIT_FORM, then behaviour will correspond to the parameter chosen by the designer. This may be as shown in Table 5.4.

**Table 5.4 Arguments used with EXIT_FORM**

| Argument | Function |
|---|---|
| ASK_COMMIT* | The operator is prompted to commit changes during the processing of EXIT_FORM. |
| DO_COMMIT | Forms automatically validates any changes, COMMITs the current transaction, then exits the form, but *does not* ask the operator to confirm. |
| NO_COMMIT | Validation and exit, but no COMMIT and no confirmation from the operator. |
| NO_VALIDATE | Exit from the current Form only, nothing else (so no COMMIT, validation, or prompt). |

*Default Value.

## POST

POST;

This function writes data to the database from the Form application but will refrain from actuating a COMMIT in the database. SQL*Forms will validate the Form upon receiving the POST command, then if there are changes to post to the database, the data in the Form will be read block by block and INSERTed, UPDATEd, or DELETEd from the base tables in the database.

Any data that the designer has arranged to be POSTed to the database will be stored upon the next COMMIT: effectively, in SQL*Forms, this will mean the COMMIT_FORM packaged procedure or the operator's operation of the COMMIT key. The CLEAR_FORM Packaged Procedure will effect a ROLLBACK within Forms, if COMMIT is inappropriate.

# CLEAR_FORM( )

CLEAR_FORM;
CLEAR_FORM(*comm_option*);
CLEAR_FORM(*comm_option*, TO_SAVEPOINT);
CLEAR_FORM(*comm_option*, FULL_ROLLBACK);

This packaged procedure is very similar to the V2 Macro of the same functionality (CLRFRM) in its simplest form: it is designed simply to flush out the current Form (the Form in which it appears). At this simplest level, CLEAR_FORM will prompt the operator to commit any changes made during the preceding transaction if any work has been done that has not been posted or committed. If a ROLLBACK is used in PL/SQL code in Forms, it will function as though the CLEAR_FORM packaged procedure had been stated instead, but with no parameters specified.

Alternatively, the designer may supply arguments that determine how CLEAR_FORM will operate. For example:

```
CLEAR_FORM(NO_VALIDATE, TO_SAVEPOINT);
```

See Table 5.5.

**Table 5.5 Arguments used with CLEAR_FORM**

| Argument | Function |
|---|---|
| ASK_COMMIT* | The operator is prompted to commit changes during the processing of CLEAR_FORM. |
| DO_COMMIT | Forms automatically validates any changes, COMMITs the current transaction, then flushes out the form, but *does not* ask the operator to confirm. |
| NO_COMMIT | Validation and flushing, but no COMMIT and no confirmation from the operator. |
| NO_VALIDATE | Flushing only, nothing else. |
| TO_SAVEPOINT* (for use in a called Form) | All uncommitted changes (including changes that have been POSTed but not committed) in the current transaction are ROLLED BACK to what Oracle describe as 'the current Form's savepoint'. *It is not clear precisely what this means,* but it may be surmised that ROLLBACK reverses changes to the savepoint generated by a CALL or NEW_FORM, or to a savepoint generated in some other fashion in the current transaction. |
| FULL_ROLLBACK (for use in a called Form) | All uncommitted changes, including any posted, but uncommitted data, that were made during the current Forms runtime session will be ROLLED BACK. This option cannot be specified for a Form that has been set to run in POST-Only mode. |

*Default Values Assumed if arguments not specified.

# COMMIT_FORM

COMMIT_FORM;

This procedure will perform a type of COMMIT operation: it will ensure that data in the database matches data contained in the Form. The following actions occur when this procedure is invoked:

- The Form is Validated;
- For each block:
  Post (if appropriate);
  Delete (if deletes exist);
  Insert (if inserts exist);
  Update (if updates exist);
  COMMIT;
- Release all table and row locks held by the operator.

The COMMIT statement used in PL/SQL in SQL*Forms will take these actions when parsed during runtime.

# CLEAR_BLOCK( )

CLEAR_BLOCK;
CLEAR_BLOCK(*parameter*);

Like the Clear Block function key, this Packaged Procedure will flush to current block in the Form. If there are any changes that should be COMMITed or POSTed, then the procedure can change its behaviour if a parameter is specified. For example:

```
CLEAR_BLOCK(NO_COMMIT);
```

Table 5.6 specifies parameters.

**Table 5.6 Parameters explained**

| Parameter | Explanation |
|---|---|
| ASK_COMMIT | An Alert Box will appear, prompting the Operator to COMMIT or ROLLBACK the changes. |
| DO_COMMIT | Changes will be validated; a COMMIT will be performed; and the current block will be flushed out, but *without prompting the operator.* |
| NO_COMMIT | Changes will be validated and the current block flushed, but the operator will not be prompted. |
| NO_VALIDATE | Only a flush occurs, nothing else. |

# CLEAR_EOL, CLEAR_FIELD, CLEAR_RECORD

```
CLEAR_EOL;
CLEAR_FIELD;
CLEAR_RECORD;
```

The following three commands are for clearing out ('flushing') their respective objects:#

*_EOL* Clears to the 'End Of Line' in the current field, or to the end of the line in the current scroll region. 'Current' is the position of the cursor.

*_FIELD* For the current field, clears out the entire field, rather than just one line in a scroll region, and sets its content to *NULL.*

*_RECORD* Clears out (flushes) the current record. Oracle says that 'If a query is open in the block, SQL*Forms fetches a record to refill the block'. This seems a little odd in this context since no trigger can fire while a Form is in Query Mode! Presumably, this relates to the internal processing of a SQL*Forms query and operator 'viewing mode', therefore: the manual's flow chart indicates that this actually means something like 'display the next sequential record from those retrieved already', rather than actually implying a fetch from the database's base table.

# DEFAULT_VALUE( )

DEFAULT_VALUE('*value*', '*form_field*');
DEFAULT_VALUE('*value*', 'GLOBAL.*variable*');

This function copies the <*value*> given into the <*form_field*> or GLOBAL variable indicated if the current value of the variable is NULL. In the case where the variable contains a non-null current value, DEFAULT_VALUE will not function at all. For example:

```
DEFAULT_VALUE('1000', 'global.totaliser');
DEFAULT_VALUE('1000', ':global.totaliser');
```

If the variable is a GLOBAL variable that has not been defined, then SQL*Forms will automatically define the variable named.

# COPY_REGION, CUT_REGION, PASTE_REGION

COPY_REGION;
CUT_REGION;
PASTE_REGION;

These three Packaged Procedures are designed to operate upon text displayed in fields on the screen. The user must first mark a 'region'—an area of text—using the [select] key. The region can then be CUT out, or copied (COPY) using CUT_REGION or COPY_REGION as required.

*COPY_* Will place the contents of the text buffer at the current cursor position.

*CUT_* Will remove ('cut out') the text that has been marked by the operator, placing it in the text buffer.

*PASTE_* Will paste the contents of the editor buffer into the field in which the cursor is currently sitting, pasting from the point at which the cursor is currently, onwards.

# DISPLAY_FIELD( )

DISPLAY_FIELD(*fieldname*, *display_attribute*);

This Procedure is designed to allow modification of the physical display attributes of a field. The modification can be to any field, including the current one. The attributes available will vary from platform to platform, and are based upon those attributes available for definition by the Oracle*Terminal product.

For example, the designer may want a field to change to emboldened text in order to highlight its content, or underlined text to prevent it standing out in a full screen.

```
DISPLAY_FIELD('b1.surname', 'BOLD');
DISPLAY_FIELD('b1.cursal', 'UNDERLINE');
```

Common attributes are as follows:

NORMAL
UNDERLINE
BOLD
INVERSE
BOLD-UNDERLINE
INVERSE-UNDERLINE
BOLD-INVERSE
BOLD-INVERSE-UNDERLINE

- Once a field has been set with DISPLAY_FIELD, the setting will remain thus until another call to the function is made. This may happen when the ENTER_QUERY Packaged Procedure is run or key pressed, for example.
- Any field in the current Form may be referenced, but not a field in any other Form.
- Only the current instance of the referenced field will be adjusted, so references to fields in multi-record blocks will only become effective for the current record upon which Forms is 'working'.
- Changes will last only for the duration of the current runtime session.

# SET_FIELD( )

SET_FIELD(*fieldname*, *argument*, ATTR_ON);
SET_FIELD(*fieldname*, *argument*, ATTR_OFF);

SET_FIELD allows the designer to re-specify a field, or series of fields' attributes dynamically at runtime, and is thoroughly revolutionary in relation to any Forms 2.2 or 2.3 functionality! The <*argument*> determines which attribute is changed for which <*fieldname*> in the current Form.

```
SET_FIELD('b1.salary', DISPLAYED, ATTR_OFF);
SET_FIELD('b1.manager', UPDATE_NULL, ATTR_ON);
```

The attributes are set on with the ATTR_ON switch; off with the ATTR_OFF switch (see Table 5.7).

**Table 5.7 Arguments and field attributes**

| Argument | Field attribute |
|---|---|
| AUTO_HELP | Automatic Hint |
| AUTO_SKIP | Automatic Skip |
| DISPLAYED | Displayed on Screen |
| ECHO | Echoed to Screen |
| ENTERABLE | Input Allowed |
| FIXED_LENGTH | Fixed Length |
| QUERYABLE | Query Allowed |
| REQUIRED | Required (Mandatory) |
| UPDATE_NULL | Update If Null |
| UPDATEABLE | Update Allowed |
| UPPER_CASE | Uppercase |

- Only one attribute can be set for one field at a time, though there may be many different SET_FIELD statements for the same field.
- Once an attribute has been changed, it will remain changed until it is reset by another statement, but only during the runtime of the Form.
- By default, the ATTR_ON switch is assumed, but it will be safest, and most accurate for debugging purposes, always to state whether_ON or_OFF is intended.
- Any change may be made to any field in the Form: this looks a little odd if fields suddenly vanish as they become non-display! *The designer should take care to avoid silly operations such as trying to make the current field Non-display.* Obviously, the cursor could not legally be sitting in the field were this to happen!

- No field on Page Zero may be affected using SET_FIELD.
- The current field cannot be made non-display.
- If INPUT_ALLOWED is OFF, a field cannot be made either UPDATEABLE or UPDATE_NULL.
- A field that is not displayed cannot be made QUERYABLE.
- A field that has had its ENTERABLE, UPDATE_ALLOWED, or UPDATE_NULL attribute set, cannot be made REQUIRED.
- There is no implicit validation following an attribute change, and validation of a field's contents will not happen until validation would occur normally or programmatically during runtime.
- Additional changes that would normally occur at design time will 'propagate' through a field's attributes logically. For example, if a previously displayed field has its DISPLAYED attribute switched off, SQL*Forms will automatically disable UPDATEABLE, UPDATE_NULL, REQUIRED, and QUERYABLE attributes.

# EDIT_FIELD( )

EDIT_FIELD;
EDIT_FIELD(*x_pos*, *y_pos*, *width*, *height*);

Rather like the Field Editor key, this Procedure will open a field editing pop-up for the current field, then place the Form in Edit mode. The parameters, <*x_pos*> and <*y_pos*> allow the designer to specify the location of the top left-hand corner of the edit window; while the <*width*> and <*height*> parameters enable specification of the width and height of the window in terms of screen columns and rows, respectively.

For example, to form a pop-up window the coordinates for the top left-hand corner of which are *x*=45, *y*=15, and with a size of 10 screen columns by 10 screen rows, the following command could be entered:

```
EDIT_FIELD(45, 15, 10, 10);
```

The adjustment of the size of the edit pop-up is entirely independent of the default size that would be produced based upon the width or datatype of the field for which the pop-up has appeared, so a large, impressive pop-up can be defined, even for a small field! If the parameters are not defined, SQL*Forms will, as with the [edit field] key, determine the width, height, and co-ordinate positions by default.

## The art and architecture of Pages

It is important to understand the philosophy behind SQL*Forms Pages before continuing to look at their implementation, since Oracle terminology here is somewhat strange. It should be understood from the outset that there is no need to make the use of pages any more complex than need be, all the additional features discussed here are available, but are not necessarily recommended, and are certainly not appropriate for every application.

> Pages can be quite straightforward, and need use none of the special settings available unless an application specifically requires them.

In SQL*Forms, therefore, a page may be two things. First, a Page may be a straightforward Forms screen containing text, graphics and fields. Second, a Page may be a pop-up 'window', or 'view' onto an area of text, graphics, and fields, known as a 'POP-UP' page. In the second case, then, in Forms 3, a page may be larger than the physical screen, up to 255 columns by 255 lines. Where it is thus larger, the screen can scroll horizontally or vertically to display fields and text at runtime, or any object in Painter mode.

## Pop-up Pages

Generally, in order for a page to be displayed, there must be a field placed upon it to which the cursor can jump. There is a special case, requiring the use of the SHOW_PAGE Packaged Procedure, where a Page can be directly addressed by referencing its number—this is covered later. As we have said, and as Fig. 5.1 shows, a page may be up to 255 columns by 255 lines in size and the size can be adjusted by using an attribute called *Page Size (x, y)*.

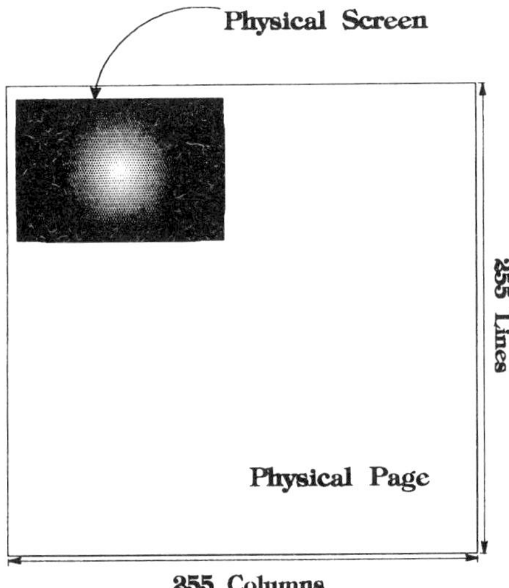


*Figure 5.1 Page dimensions.*

Now, imagine a window (view) through which any portion of a Forms page can be viewed. The window can be moved around, over the page, to display different portions of its text, graphics, and fields. The window itself has a set size, and whatever it is placed above will appear in it, like a magnifying glass being moved over a page, though, obviously, without the magnifying effect!

The size of the windowed portion of the chosen page is defined by two attributes called *View Size x* and *View Size y*; the position of the window, by the position of the top left-hand corner, the *View Page (x, y)* coordinates attribute.

> Coordinate (1, 1) is the top left-hand corner of each SQL*Forms page.

The chosen page's windowed 'view' will then appear on top of the last displayed Forms page at the coordinates defined by an attribute called, *View Loc (x, y)*. There is a special '*pop-up*' *attribute* which, if selected, will cause the window to appear on top of the last displayed page, otherwise the page will be treated as 'the new page' in the same way as earlier versions of SQL*Forms treated a new page.

# View Size, Page Size, View Page, and View Loc

Figure 5.2 shows the relationship between the attributes available for defining pop-up pages. A *Border* can be defined for a pop-up window. It may include horizontal and vertical scroll bars, a title, and an actual BORDER LINE around the pop-up view. It is important to note that if an automatic Border is used in this way it will take up some of the space defined for the size of the view itself, so the area seen through a bordered-view will be *smaller* than it would be were there no border. The same effect as the use of the Border Page Attribute can be attained by simply drawing a physical 'border' line around the view on the page designed to pop-up.

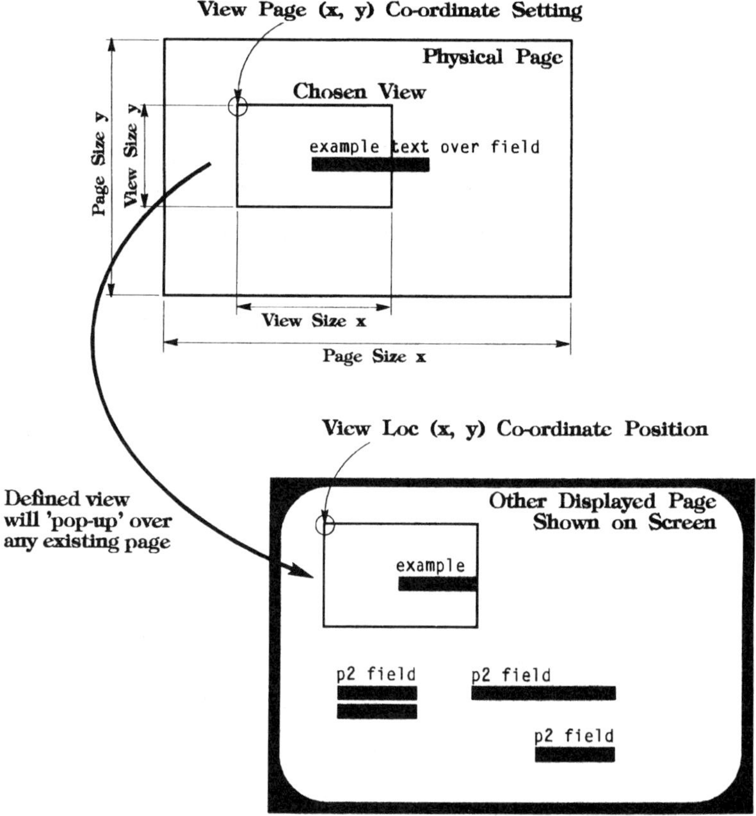


*Figure 5.2 Defining pop-up pages.*

# —Page Definition displays—

Pages, like FIELDS and BLOCKS, have their own adjustment screens, thus:

- *Page Definition Form* Shows details for one page only, in a Dialogue Box.
- *Page Definition Spread Table* Shows details of one page in relation to all others in the current Form.

The two versions of the screen are shown in Figs 5.3 and 5.4 on page 100. The [change display type] function key is used to swap between them.

Notice that the scroll bar at the bottom of the Spread Table Version screen will display the relationship of the currently displayed panel to the other available panels. Since this is the first, the block of shading is to the left-hand side of the scroll bar. Table 5.8 lists the Pop-up page attributes.

**Table 5.8 Pop-up page attributes**

| Pop-up page attribute | Description |
|---|---|
| *Page Number* | Absolute reference label for this page. |
| *Pop up* | If selected, this page will appear on top of the last displayed page. If the page size is smaller than the size of the screen page, it will appear as though this page had 'popped up' at a point on the page. |
| *Page Size* (Do not change unless specifically necessary! The default will be perfectly satisfactory.) | The height and width of the page. In Forms 3, a page may be up to 255 columns by 255 rows. A page that is larger than the VDU screen can display will scroll horizontally and vertically in screen painter mode, or in operator mode, where the cursor will jump to each field, displaying the portion of page upon which it is sitting. *Can be left blank to set the default (usually around 22 x 24.)* |
| *View Size* | The size of the area that will be displayed. *x* defines the horizontal attribute, the width; *y* defines the vertical attribute, the height. |
| *View Loc* | Location on the last displayed page of the top left-hand corner of the portion of this pop-up page that will be displayed, the size of which is defined by the 'View Size' setting. *View Loc defines the position of the view on the screen.* |
| *View Page* | The position of the top left-hand corner of the view chosen from the pop-up page in terms of co-ordinates on that physical page. *View Page defines the position of the view on the page.* |
| *Border* | The pop-up has a single line drawn around it when it appears, using the system's standard line-draw character. Note: border characters are included in the specified size of the view, to prevent this addition overwriting extra characters on the underlying page when the view 'pops up'. |
| *Vertical Scroll Bar* | A vertically positioned scroll bar appears at the left of the window. |
| *Horizontal Scroll Bar* | A horizontally aligned scroll bar appears at the bottom of the window. |
| *Remove on Exit* | Ensures that the current pop-up page will disappear when the cursor moves out of it. *This attribute will only work if two pages are on screen simultaneously*—usually where one underlies the other. |
| *Title:* | Accepts any text desired by the designer. This will form a title for the pop-up window. The text will be centred automatically within the width of the window. A title will be ignored unless the border attribute is selected also. Note: title border characters are included in the specified size of the view, to prevent this addition overwriting extra characters on the underlying page when the view 'pops up'. Therefore, less of the content of the window will be visible than if there were no title. |

```
Action  foRm  Block  Field  Trigger  Procedure  Image  Help  Options
                          Page Definition
 Page                  Pg Sz  Pg Sz  Vw Sz  Vw Sz  Vw Lc  Vw Lc  Vw Pg  V
 Number    Pop Up        X      Y      X      Y      X      Y      X
 1         [   ]
                                                                        >
Enter the page number of the page.
Frm: PERSON      Blk: b1      Fld: INCEP      Trg:               <Rep>
```

Figure 5.3 Page Definition Spread Table.

```
Action  foRm  Block  Field  Trigger  Procedure  Image  Help  Options
                          Page Definition

   Page Number: 1                      [   ] Pop Up

   Page Size: X:       Y:              [   ] Border
   View Size: X:       Y:              [   ] Vertical Scroll Bar
   View Loc:  X:       Y:              [   ] Horizontal Scroll Bar
   View Page: X:       Y:              [   ] Remove on Exit

   Title:

Enter the page number of the page.
Frm: PERSON      Blk: b1      Fld: INCEP      Trg:               <Rep>
```

Figure 5.4 Page Definition Dialogue Box.

# Page View control

ANCHOR_VIEW(*page_number*, *x_pos*, *y_pos*);
MOVE_VIEW(*page_number*, *x_pos*, *y_pos*);
RESIZE_VIEW(*page_number*, ***width***, ***height***);

These three Procedures allow the designer to control a Page View. Remember that the coordinates of the view are optionally specified by the designer for each pop-up page (even for non-pop-ups) when the page is defined in SQL*Forms. <*page_number*> specifies the numeric identifier of the referenced page, its Page Number. <*x_pos*> and <*y_pos*> specify a location in terms of screen columns and screen rows, respectively. <*width*> and <*height*> in RESIZE_ specify a width in screen columns and a height in screen rows, respectively.

The following commands move the Location of the view of Page-13 to (1, 1) when it pops up; adjust the position on Page-13 that forms the top left-hand corner of the area that will be viewed as a pop-up to (20, 20); and specify that the area that will be seen by the operator measures 80 columns by 6 screen rows high:

```
ANCHOR_VIEW(13, 1, 1);
MOVE_VIEW(13, 20, 20);
RESIZE_VIEW(13, 80, 6);
```

Remember that a 'View' is a page or subdivision of a page that has been chosen by the designer to appear on top of another Forms page. The settings have particularly silly names because they only confuse the issue: 'ANCHOR_VIEW' may quite happily be called 'NEW_VIEWLOC', for example, but it is not. Only 'RESIZE_VIEW' seems appropriate.

*ANCHOR_* Moves the *view of a page* to a new position on screen, thus changing the point at which the view appears for the operator. This adjusts the *View Loc(x, y)* coordinate for the pop-up page.

*MOVE_* Moves a view of a page to a *new position on that page,* thus changing the *part of the page that is seen by the operator,* but not its *position* on screen. This adjusts the *View Page(x, y)* coordinate for the pop-up page.

*RESIZE_* Adjusts the *area of the page that is seen by the operator* through the pop-up view window. An increase in size using RESIZE_VIEW therefore shows more of the pop-up window, showing more of the pop-up page through it. This adjusts the *View Size (x, y)* setting for the pop-up page.

## Page Display control

DISPLAY_PAGE(*page_number*, *argument*);
HIDE_PAGE(*page_number*);
SHOW_PAGE(*page_number*);

These three Procedures are quite straightforward: they merely take as the principal argument the page number of the page concerned.

*DISPLAY_* Takes the name of a page display attribute as its <*argument*> value. Unfortunately, these are wholly device- and platform-specific, but their details are available by using the Oracle*Terminal product which contains mappings for individual attributes. These can be referenced and adjusted by the designer or by the DBA, according to system permissions.

*HIDE_* Will make the page in <*page_number*> vanish. The assumption is that this is a pop-up page displayed on screen already, so HIDE_PAGE is a clear-up or specification command. Useful for context-sensitive screen pop-ups.

*SHOW_* Will display the page specified in <*page_number*> on screen. It should be noted that even though the page appears *it is not made active* by SQL*Forms, and the designer should be wary of trying to retrieve records into a block whose fields are displayed in this way: the NU must be moved down into the Block for this to happen! There's no magic here, everything works as you would normally expect a block to work. *SHOW_PAGE should only be used for pop-up pages.* If pages on-screen overlap (this can occur in bit-mapped GUI-type systems especially), then the page that has been displayed most recently using SHOW_PAGE will appear underneath the currently active page (unless it has immediately become the active page), but on top of any other pop-up pages.

# Designer tip: automatic pages —and SYNCHRONIZE—

SYNCHRONIZE;

SYNCHRONIZE is a Packaged Procedure that is almost impossible to explain straightforwardly, and most manuals on the subject fail dismally. The command is intended to make the displayed version of what is going on coincide with the internal state of a SQL*Forms program (application). In other words, the operator can see exactly what is happening at a point in time. George Koch says in his book, *ORACLE The Complete Reference* (McGraw-Hill-Osborne, New York, 1990) '...forces SQL*Forms to display any normal screen information that it should write to the screen but hasn't yet,' which is about as close as it is possible to get to an accurate definition of the functionality of SYNCHRONIZE. The point of explaining SYNCHRONIZE at all is that *it allows the designer to force SQL*Forms to operate like a 3GL and display things when expected, which it does not do by nature.* The following example code produces the startling effect of making a pop-up page appear, followed by another, followed by another, and can be used as the basis for further intriguing research into SQL*Forms. The FOR LOOP is used for timing only, so it contains a NULL to make the compiler happy.

```
SQL*FORMS_VERSION = 3.0.16.5.1
TERSE = ON
DEFINE FORM
   NAME = P_PROC_TEST
   TITLE = p_proc_test
   DEFAULT_MENU_APPLICATION = DEFAULT
   DEFINE TRIGGER
      NAME = PRE-FORM
      TRIGGER_TYPE = V3
      TEXT = <<<
      SHOW_PAGE(1);
      synchronize;
            FOR I IN 1..8000 LOOP
               NULL;
            END LOOP;
      synchronize;
      SHOW_PAGE(2);
      synchronize;
            FOR I IN 1..8000 LOOP
```

```
                NULL;
            END LOOP;
    synchronize;
    SHOW_PAGE(3);
    synchronize;
            FOR I IN 1..8000 LOOP
                NULL;
            END LOOP;
    synchronize;
    SHOW_PAGE(4);
    synchronize;
            FOR I IN 1..8000 LOOP
                NULL;
            END LOOP;
    synchronize;
    SHOW_PAGE(5);
    synchronize;
            FOR I IN 1..8000 LOOP
                NULL;
            END LOOP;
    synchronize;
    >>>
  ENDDEFINE TRIGGER
```

# ERASE( )

ERASE(*global_variable*);

Erases the GLOBAL variable the name of which is specified in the argument, <*global_variable*>, releasing the memory space that it and its content occupied. For example:

```
ERASE(':global.skill_identifier');
ERASE('global.skill_identifier');
```

# DO_KEY( )

DO_KEY('*key_packaged_procedure*');

SQL*Forms will run the code associated with the Key-Level Trigger the name of which appears in the argument, <*'key_packaged_procedure'*>. If no trigger code exists for the specified key, Forms will actuate the function that the key would perform.

This rather peculiar Packaged Procedure was originally designed to be used with the SQL*Menu product, in order to mimic SQL*Forms operation within a menu. For example:

```
DO_KEY('duplicate_record');
DO_KEY('edit_field');
```

<*'key_packaged_procedure'*> can take the name of any Key-Level Trigger available in SQL*Forms Version 3.0. Remember! Using this Packaged Procedure is the long way around! All the other Packaged Procedures are already available to perform operations such as DUPLICATE_FIELD, or whatever.

# ENTER_QUERY( )

**ENTER_QUERY;**
**ENTER_QUERY(ALL_RECORDS);**
ENTER_QUERY(ALL_RECORDS, FOR_UPDATE);
ENTER_QUERY(ALL_RECORDS, FOR_UPDATE, NOWAIT);
**ENTER_QUERY(FOR_UPDATE);**
ENTER_QUERY(FOR_UPDATE, NOWAIT);

The default Packaged Procedure takes no arguments. It will flush the current block, placing the Form into Query Mode. Prior to this, if there are any changes that need to be COMMITted, SQL*Forms will prompt the operator with the appropriate Alert Box. The other options will adjust the Procedure's response as shown in Table 5.9.

**Table 5.9 Options to adjust the Procedure's response**

| Option | Function |
|---|---|
| ALL_RECORDS | When the EXECUTE_QUERY key or Packaged Procedure is executed, SQL*Forms *will retrieve* all records (rows) from the Block's Base Table. |
| ALL_RECORDS, FOR_UPDATE | When the EXECUTE_QUERY key or Packaged Procedure is executed, SQL*Forms *will retrieve* all records (rows) from the Block's Base Table *and Forms will attempt to lock all the records* selected thus immediately. |
| FOR_UPDATE | When the EXECUTE_QUERY key or Packaged Procedure is executed, SQL*Forms will *attempt to lock all the records* selected thus immediately. |
| NOWAIT | If this parameter is used, if SQL*Forms is unable to acquire a lock on all the selected records, it will issue a message in the Status Line, '`Attempting to reserve record for update or delete (CTRL-C to cancel)...`' and will continue to try to acquire the lock. *When NOWAIT is not specified,* Forms will attempt to acquire the lock but the operator has no override facility at all, and must wait until the lock is acquired before further operations can continue. |

Important: it is *not* recommended that the FOR_UPDATE and ALL_RECORDS options are used without very careful consideration! Both these options can cause the current user process to acquire many resources and make heavy utilization of the Oracle system and operating platform, especially where there are thousands, millions, or billions of records in the database.

# EXECUTE_QUERY( )

**EXECUTE_QUERY;**
**EXECUTE_QUERY(ALL_RECORDS);**
EXECUTE_QUERY(ALL_RECORDS, FOR_UPDATE);
EXECUTE_QUERY(ALL_RECORDS, FOR_UPDATE, NOWAIT);
**EXECUTE_QUERY(FOR_UPDATE);**
EXECUTE_QUERY(FOR_UPDATE, NOWAIT);

EXECUTE_QUERY will flush the current block, open a Query, and fetch records, either as specified by some preceding process or according to the options specified (if an argument is given.) These are detailed in Table 5.10. If there are changes to COMMIT before the Procedure is run, then the operator will be prompted for them by the appropriate Alert Box.

**Table 5.10 Options available with EXECUTE_QUERY**

| Option | Function |
|---|---|
| ALL_RECORDS | Forms will flush the current block, open a Query, and fetch *all* the records from the Block's Base Table. If there are changes to commit, the operator will be prompted for them prior to these actions. |
| ALL_RECORDS, FOR_UPDATE | SQL*Forms will flush the current block, open a Query, and *will retrieve* all records (rows) from the Block's Base Table, then *attempting to LOCK all the records* selected thus immediately. |
| FOR_UPDATE | SQL*Forms will *attempt to lock all the records* selected immediately and execute the query as above. |
| NOWAIT | If this parameter is used, if SQL*Forms is unable to acquire a lock on all the selected records, it will issue a message in the Status Line, '`Attempting to reserve record for update or delete (CTRL-C to cancel)...`' and will continue to try to acquire the lock. *When NOWAIT is not specified,* Forms will attempt to acquire the lock but the operator has no override facility at all, and must wait until the lock is acquired before further operations can continue. |

Important: it is *not* recommended that the FOR_UPDATE and ALL_RECORDS options are used without very careful consideration! Both these options can cause the current user process to acquire many resources and make heavy utilization of the Oracle system and operating platform, especially where there are thousands, millions, or billions of records in the database.

## GO_place( )

GO_BLOCK(*'blockname'*);
GO_FIELD(*'fieldname'*);
GO_RECORD(*relative_number*);

These three Procedures are used for navigating to the chosen object. GO_BLOCK and GO_FIELD simply take the name of the object referenced. It is up to the designer to ensure that the name of the object is uniquely specified.

GO_RECORD, however, takes an integer (whole number) that specifies a record, relative to the first displayed in the current block. The *<relative_number>* argument may also be an expression that evaluates to an integer. GO_RECORD is designed to be used with values derived from SYSTEM.cursor_record and SYSTEM.trigger_record, or to take a derived integer or programmed integer, according to application requirements. For example:

```
GO_BLOCK('vehicle_details');
GO_FIELD('vehicle_details.v_registration');
GO_RECORD(to_number(:SYSTEM.cursor_record) + 6);
```

## HOST( )

HOST(*'operating_system_level_command'*);
HOST(*'operating_system_level_command'*, NO_SCREEN);

HOST is a 'traditional' facility in SQL*Forms: it takes an argument that may be any operating system-level command allowed on the current operating platform. Some examples follow.

The NO_SCREEN switch will prevent SQL*Forms from clearing the screen and prompting the operator to return from the command, which it does by default. For example:

- *Running a SQL*Plus sales report*

  ```
  HOST('SQLPLUS -SILENT joanna/bicycle @salesrep.sql');
  ```

- *Running a dynamically chosen SQL*Plus report*

```
declare
  usr char(30) := '';
  pass char(30) := '';
  rept char(10) := '';
begin
  usr  :=  user;
  pass :=  :global.password;
  rept :=  :b1.repname;
  /*  Actually, these variables could be used    */
  /*  directly here, but they are left out for   */
  /*  simplicity in the statement below.         */
  host('sqlplus -s '||usr||'/'||pass||' @'||rept);
end;
```

- *Producing a current directory listing in UNIX*

```
HOST('ls -l');
```

- *Printing out a VMS file using a local system PRINT utility*

```
HOST('print helptext01.txt;1 /lineprinter');
```

- *Producing a SQL*ReportWriter report, sent to a File*

```
HOST('RUNREP REPORT=recruit USERID=joe/smirnoff
DESTYPE=file DESNAME=RECRUIT.LIS');
```

# USER_EXIT( )

USER_EXIT(*'exit_string_detail'*);
USER_EXIT(*'exit_string_detail'*, *'error_message_string'*);

A 'User Exit' is a call to a piece of code written in a Pro*Oracle language pre-compiler, such as Pro*C, Pro*Fortran, Pro*Pascal, Pro*Ada, or Pro*PL/1, or in a non-Oracle language (C, COBOL, etc.). Pro* languages enable ESQL (Embedded Structured Query Language) commands to be included in them so that they can make use of the data maintained by the current Oracle Instance. The idea is to combine the power, flexibility and speed of a Third-Generation Language with the sophisticated data storage capabilities of a Relational Database Management System. <*'exit_string_detail'*> will be the name of the User Exit called by this Packaged Procedure. The <*'error_message_string'*> argument can take a string that will print out if the User Exit call fails.

Setting up User Exits is not a simple process, though it is well known and straightforward. This area is outside the scope of this book, and readers are referred to the relevant manuals on their Pro* language of choice or, for further detailed information on how User Exits relate to SQL*Forms Version 3, to the *Oracle SQL*Forms Designer's Reference Version 3.0,* Oracle Part No. 3304-V3.0 0191.

## LIST_VALUES( )

LIST_VALUES(NO_RESTRICT);
LIST_VALUES(RESTRICT);

This Packaged Procedure will run the code that displays the List of Values for the current field. This may be set to V2 or V3, according to the type of implementation chosen by the designer. The List of Values will remain displayed until the operator presses the [exit/cancel] key, or selects a value that will appear in the field. By default, the NO_RESTRICT parameter is used by the Procedure. This inhibits the use of the SQL*Forms Automatic Search and Complete (ASC) facility.

ASC will take any non-NULL value that has been placed in the field by the operator and assume that it is intended to restrict the search list displayed in the LOV produced for the field. The non-NULL value is taken to be a search criterion. If the restricted list that would be produced is of one item in length, SQL*Forms will automatically read the value into the field as though the operator had selected it, otherwise the restricted list is printed out in the LOV format selected during design (either V2 or V3). RESTRICT forces SQL*Forms to assume that ASC will be used, and to act accordingly.

## MESSAGE( )

MESSAGE(*'message_text_string'*);

This Procedure will print out the content of the <*'message_text_string'*> in the message line at the bottom of the screen for the operator. Provided that they evaluate to a purely CHARACTER argument, any series of elements may be concatenated in the MESSAGE parameter. The TO_CHAR function (SQL and PL/SQL) can be used to convert, say, a numeric variable's value, into a character value for output. For example:

```
MESSAGE('FUR-40666: Only Small AND Furry animals are
allowed.');
MESSAGE('Max. Bonus was= '||to_char(:b1.bonus));
```

Note: if TO_CHAR is performed upon a variable or expression that would yield a character output anyway, SQL*Forms will yield a peculiar message that seems to relate to over-use of the function: '...: `too many declarations of` *{whatever}* `match this call`.' which in fact relates to this problem and not to mis-specification!

CHAPTER SIX

# PACKAGED FUNCTIONS

## Introduction

Packaged Functions are PL/SQL functions that are available to the systems designer in SQL*Forms Version 3. They are principally designed to enable an operating attribute of or information about an object in the currently running Form to be returned to a calling function for use in a conditional or other statement that enhances application processing. Packaged Functions can also fruitfully be used in debugging, since they will indicate the status of different elements during a runtime session.

Remember that a Packaged Function is just that—a function, not a command, so it will return a datum for processing, rather than performing any action of its own.

## APPLICATION_ and FORM_CHARACTERISTIC

APPLICATION_CHARACTERISTIC(CALLING_FORM)
APPLICATION_CHARACTERISTIC(CURRENT_FORM)
FORM_CHARACTERISTIC(FIRST_BLOCK)
FORM_CHARACTERISTIC(LAST_BLOCK)

**APPLICATION_CHARACTERISTIC** returns a *CHARACTER VALUE* that corresponds with the name of the calling Form, if the current Form has been called from another (CALLING_FORM) or of the current Form (CURRENT_FORM). This function is particularly useful where a Form may be called from many different Forms (perhaps it is a menu) or where a piece of code for a Form-Level Procedure is being written, where that Procedure will be used in several different Forms applications.

**FORM_CHARACTERISTIC** returns a *CHARACTER VALUE* that indicates the name of the first block in the current Form (FIRST_BLOCK) or the last block in the current Form (LAST_BLOCK). In either case, the definition of 'first' and 'last' is relative to the *sequence number* assigned to the block during the creation of the Form by the designer. For example,

```
IF APPLICATION_CHARACTERISTIC(CALLING_FORM) = 'STAFF_DETAIL'
    THEN MESSAGE ('Upon EXIT you will return to the STAFF
      Form...');
ELSIF APPLICATION_CHARACTERISTIC(CALLING_FORM) = 'MENU_A1'
    THEN MESSAGE('Upon EXIT you will return to the Main
      Menu...');
END IF;
```

# FORM_FAILURE, _FATAL, _SUCCESS

FORM_FATAL
FORM_FAILURE
FORM_SUCCESS

These three functions test the outcome of the most recent action to determine a status that will be returned to the calling statement. They will return a BOOLEAN VALUE of TRUE or FALSE. Since it is assumed that the reader is already familiar with these concepts, the definitions of 'SUCCESS', 'FAILURE' and 'FATAL ERROR' are only given *roughly* here, as follows:

*SUCCESS:* A DML Statement acts upon at least one row (SELECT, INSERT, UPDATE, DELETE).

*FAILURE:* A DML Statement fails to act upon at least one row.

*FATAL:* A SQL*Forms command causes the Host Operating System to run out of memory.

Table 6.1 shows what happens according to each type of function and the status it determines. Note: it is important that the statement that invokes one of these status-returning functions is the FIRST ACTION performed by a piece of SQL*Forms code after the tested event, otherwise the designer could be testing the wrong event! For example:

```
...
if FORM_FAILURE = TRUE then error_code_routine_1;
elsif FORM_FATAL = TRUE then
   message('Urgent! Call User Support... ERR-X3jk7');
end if;
...
```

**Table 6.1 Functions and their outcome**

| Function used | Boolean value returned | | |
|---|---|---|---|
| | On 'Success' | On 'Failure' | On 'Fatal' |
| *FORM_SUCCESS* | TRUE | FALSE | FALSE |
| *FORM_FAILURE* | FALSE | TRUE | FALSE |
| *FORM_FATAL* | FALSE | FALSE | TRUE |

# BLOCK_ CHARACTERISTIC( )

BLOCK_CHARACTERISTIC('*blockname*', *parameter*)

BLOCK_CHARACTERISTIC will return information of the type <*parameter*> about the block specified by <*blockname*>. The datum returned to the calling statement will be of *CHARACTER datatype.* The <*parameter*> argument may be *one* of the types per function call shown in Table 6.2.

**Table 6.2 Parameters and their returns**

| Parameter | Returns |
|---|---|
| BASE_TABLE | Name of the Base Table of this block, or NULL. |
| ENTERABLE | TRUE if the block is enterable; FALSE if not. |
| FIRST_FIELD* | Name of field with sequence number 1 in the block. |
| LAST_FIELD* | Name of the field with the highest sequence number. |
| NEXTBLOCK | Name of the next sequential block, or NULL if none. |
| PREVIOUSBLOCK | Name of the previous sequential block, or NULL. |
| RECORDS_DISPLAYED | Number of Records this block can display at once. |
| TOP_RECORD | Sequential number of the top-most record visible. |

*Only returns the field name, without including the block's name.

# FIELD_ CHARACTERISTIC( )

FIELD_CHARACTERISTIC(*'fieldname'*, *parameter*)

Where BLOCK_CHARACTERISTIC returns information about a designated BLOCK this function returns information about a specified FIELD. Since field attributes can be numerous, the function has a bewildering array of different parameters. These are listed in Table 6.3. Note that the datum returned to the calling statement will be of *CHARACTER datatype*.

**Table 6.3 Field attribute parameters and returns**

| Parameter | Returns* |
|---|---|
| AUTO_HELP | TRUE if Automatic Hint is switched on. |
| AUTO_SKIP | TRUE if Automatic Skip is switched on. |
| BASE_TABLE | TRUE if there is a Base Table. |
| DATATYPE | Returns name of the datatype. |
| DISPLAYED | TRUE if field is Displayed. |
| DISPLAY_LENGTH | Numeric length is returned as for Display Length attribute for this field. |
| ECHO | TRUE if entered values are echoed to the screen for this field. |
| ENTERABLE | TRUE if Input Allowed is on. |
| FIELD_LENGTH | Numeric length is returned as for Field Length attribute for this field. |
| FIXED_LENGTH | TRUE if switched on. |
| LIST | TRUE if the 'List of Values SQL Text' field contains a value. |
| NEXTFIELD | Name of the next sequential field in this block, or NULL. |
| PAGE | Number of this field's page. |
| PREVIOUSFIELD | Name of the preceding sequential field, or NULL. |
| PRIMARY_KEY | TRUE if this field has its Primary Key attribute switched on by the designer. |
| QUERY_LENGTH | Numeric Query Length of this field. |
| QUERYABLE | TRUE if Query Allowed is switched on. |
| REQUIRED | TRUE if Required is switched on. |
| UPDATEABLE | TRUE if Update Allowed is switched on. |
| UPDATE_NULL | TRUE if Update If NULL is switched on. |
| UPPER_CASE | TRUE if Uppercase is switched on. |
| X_POS | Numeric horizontal screen coordinate. |
| Y_POS | Numeric vertical screen coordinate. |

*In all the preceding cases if a Boolean value of 'TRUE' can be returned, the reverse will be 'FALSE' for the reverse of the setting found by FIELD_CHARACTERISTIC.

# ERROR_CODE, _TEXT, and _TYPE

ERROR_CODE
ERROR_TEXT
ERROR_TYPE

These three Packaged Functions have been designed to allow programmers to record, identify, or trap errors. They will also be useful in debugging and code-checking.

| | |
|---|---|
| *_CODE* | Returns a *NUMBER(5) Datatype* indicating the error number of the action most recently performed during the current Forms session. If the action has a SUCCESS status, the code will be 0. |
| *_TEXT* | Returns a *CHAR(78) Datatype* indicating the actual error text that SQL*Forms reports for the most recently performed runtime action. If the action has a SUCCESS status, the code returned will be NULL. |
| *_TYPE* | Returns a *CHAR(3) Datatype* indicating the scope of the error that occurred. If the action has SUCCESS status, the code returned will be NULL. Codes may be one of the following otherwise:<br>*FRM* A SQL*Forms Error.<br>*MNU* A SQL*Menu Error.<br>*ORA* Some form of ORACLE Error. |

As with FORM_FAILURE and other operation tests, the test with ERROR_type functions should be the *first action performed after the action to be tested,* otherwise SQL*Forms might report on the wrong action!

> NOTE: For a complete list of the SQL*Forms Runtime Error Messages and Codes, the reader is referred to APPENDIX E of the *Oracle SQL*Forms Designer's Reference Version 3.0,* Oracle Part No. 3304-V3.0 0191.

# Examples of error-testing code

## ERROR_CODE, ON-ERROR type trigger

This code traps a runtime error code when the operator presses the [duplicate field] or [duplicate record] key during record creation.

```
if ERROR_CODE = 41803 then
      message('Sorry: you'll need a record to copy
from!');
end if;
```

## ERROR_TEXT, ON-ERROR type trigger

This code traps a runtime error text when the operator presses the [duplicate field] or [duplicate record] key during record creation.

```
if ERROR_TEXT='No previous record to copy value from.'
then
      message('Sorry: you'll need a record to copy
from!');
end if;
```

## ERROR_TYPE, ON-ERROR type trigger

This code traps a serious error, and prevents a poorly designed form from running, stopping the current Form with the assumption that the operator should not store or validate any data (*not necessarily a good assumption!*).

```
call('recruit_updtr');
if ERROR_TYPE = 'FRM' then
      message('Contact Your Designer: ERR-FRM-XX1');
      EXIT_FORM(no_validate);
end if;
```

# MESSAGE_CODE, _TEXT, and _TYPE

MESSAGE_CODE
MESSAGE_TEXT
MESSAGE_TYPE

As SQL*Forms operates during runtime it will generate various different messages for the delectation of the operator. The three Packaged Functions described here will allow the designer to take account of the message based upon certain attributes.

*_CODE* Returns a *NUMBER(5) Datatype* representing the code for the type of Run Form message returned. The Function will return 0 at the beginning of a runtime session.

*_TEXT* Returns a *CHAR(78) Datatype* containing the actual message generated by SQL*Forms. The function will return NULL at the beginning of a runtime session.

*_TYPE* Returns a *CHAR(3) Datatype* containing a string that represents the type of message for the message most recently generated by SQL*Forms. The code may be of the following types:

*FRM* A SQL*Forms Message.
*MNU* A SQL*Menu Message.
*ORA* Some form of ORACLE Message.

As with FORM_FAILURE and other operation tests, the test with MESSAGE_-type functions should be the *first action performed after the message to be tested,* otherwise SQL*Forms might report on the wrong message!

> NOTE: For a complete list of the SQL*Forms Runtime Messages and Codes, the reader is referred to Appendix E of the *Oracle SQL*Forms Designer's Reference Version 3.0*, Oracle Part No. 3304-V3.0 0191.

# Examples of message-testing code

## MESSAGE_CODE, ON-MESSAGE type trigger

This code traps a runtime message code when the operator has pressed the [execute query] key after entering query criteria. Note: the 40350 message is trapped *prior* to its display in the Message Line, so the remainder of the trigger can replace the message.

```
if MESSAGE_CODE = 40350 then
      message('There are no Recruits with these
criteria.');
end if;
```

## MESSAGE_TEXT, ON-MESSAGE type trigger

This code traps a runtime message when the operator has pressed the [execute query] key after entering query criteria. Note: the '`Query caused no records to be retrieved.`' message is trapped *prior* to its display in the Message Line, so the remainder of the trigger can replace the message.

```
if MESSAGE_TEXT='Query caused no records to be retrieved.'
then
      message('There are no Recruits with these
criteria.');
end if;
```

## MESSAGE_TYPE, ON-MESSAGE type trigger

This code traps a Forms Message for use during debugging by a designer. Note that the code here will be run *before* the original message is displayed in the Message Line, so the text of the trigger effectively replaces the standard operation.

```
if MESSAGE_TYPE = 'FRM' then
      no_of_msgs_audit_frm := no_of_msgs_audit_frm + 1;
      m_logger_frm := MESSAGE_CODE;
elsif MESSAGE_TYPE = 'ORA' then
      no_of_msgs_audit_ora := no_of_msgs_audit_ora + 1;
      m_logger_ora := MESSAGE_CODE;
end if;
message('MESSAGE Encountered and LOGGED.');
```

*Special note*: SQL*Forms will quite happily display a new message in place of the message that was trapped but will definitely *not* try to trap this new message! The coding underlying Forms at this point checks automatically to see if the message that has just been output has been output by an ON-ERROR or ON-MESSAGE trigger, and bypasses the trapping code, avoiding endless loops and other possible problems.

# Using Packaged Procedures and Packaged Function NAME_IN( )

NAME_IN(*variable*)

PL/SQL alone, unlike many more mature languages, does not support indirect variable references, a fact which can easily cause some annoyance when programs fail to work for non-obvious reasons. Oracle have included in SQL*Forms Packaged Functions the NAME_IN function which provides this functionality. NAME_IN will return the *CHARACTER Datatype* content of the <*variable*> specified in its argument. The idea here is that the designer can incorporate the NAME_IN function within any clause of an expression that requires 'indirection', the ability to read a variable whose name alone is referenced within another variable. For example:

- Suppose that we want to use *just one statement* to tell SQL*Forms control where to jump within a program.
- Suppose that the *locations* to which we wish to jump are *numerous*.
- Suppose that *a field called REC_TYPE is entered by the operator,* and that its values could be NEW, UPD, or DEL, for 'New Recruit', 'Update Record', or 'Deletion Record'.
- Suppose that *we have three Blocks, NEW, UPD, and DEL,* that contain fields and triggers relevant to the work we wish to do in each. Part of the data entry tasks of the operator are to enter the key words, NEW, UPD, or DEL in the field REC_TYPE. Based upon this, we want to jump to the relevant Block. The function to achieve this will be GO_BLOCK, but we want an indirect reference, so we use NAME_IN, as follows:

```
GO_BLOCK(NAME_IN('b1.rec_type'));
```

Therefore when b1.rec_type contains NEW, control will jump to the first enterable field in the Block called NEW, etc. for UPD and DEL.

# Further indirection with NAME_IN( )

The advantage of NAME_IN is that it will also perform further and more detailed indirection, because it will evaluate the INNERMOST NAME_IN first, then work its way outwards (like a normal SQL function in a SELECT statement). The following example would evaluate thus:

```
GO_FIELD(NAME_IN(NAME_IN('b1.spider')));
```

1 The content of b1.SPIDER;
2 The content of the content of b1.SPIDER, say a field called b1.MAXIM:
3 The content of b1.MAXIM, suppose SURNAME.

So the cursor would be placed in the SURNAME field. As a summary:

| *Field* | *Content* | |
|---|---|---|
| B1.SPIDER | B1.MAXIM | found by the innermost NAME_IN; |
| B1.MAXIM | SURNAME | found by the outermost NAME_IN; |
| Surname | | JUMPED-TO FIELD. |

# Copy/Reference Object Facility

Perhaps one of the best of the new facilities offered by SQL*Forms is the Copy/Reference Object facility. It has been kept until now to mention because it is most particularly relevant in the context of Form-Level Procedures. Copy/Reference Object allows the designer to make use of a Procedure, Trigger, Page, Block, or Field in more than one application by COPYING or REFERENCING the object from the current SQL*Form. For example, there might be an ON-ERROR Procedure that has been made a standard throughout all an installation's Oracle Applications. The Procedure could be kept and maintained in one SQL*Form, then Referenced throughout all the others. Whenever a change is made to the 'Master' Procedure, this will ripple through to all other instances of the same Procedure in other Forms. A COPIED object is simply that, merely copied from one application into another, exactly like COPY and PASTE facilities in a word processor.

Note: it is *not possible* to reference the following:

- Constant Text (but may be Copied).
- Any object owned by the Current Form (but may be Copied).
- Any object owned by a Form that is not stored in the current instance of Oracle.

Figure 6.1 represents the Copy/Reference Object window that appears when the designer presses the [copy object] key from any point within a Form.

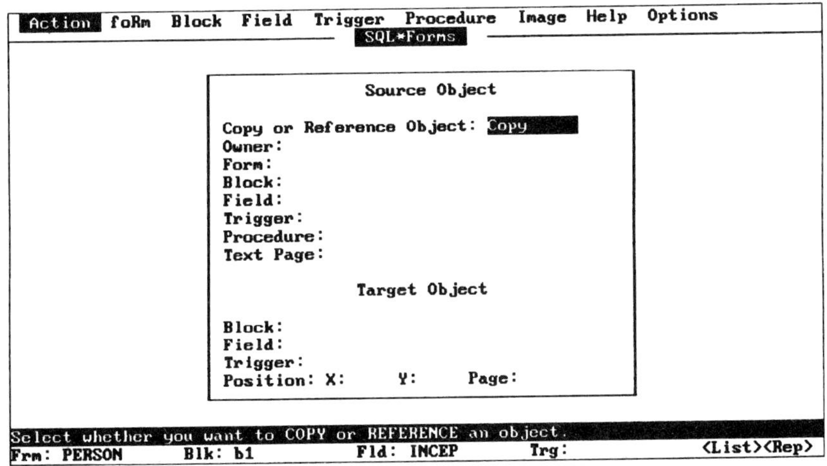


*Figure 6.1 Copy/Reference Object window.*

# Object referencing restrictions

Whenever an object is referenced from another Form, SQL*Forms places restrictions upon what is allowed to happen to the object (see Table 6.4).

**Table 6.4 Object referencing restriction summary**

| | Object type... | | | |
|---|---|---|---|---|
| **When an Object of this type is Referenced there will be...** | **Form-level Procedure** | **Block** | **Field** | **Trigger** |
| **Also referenced:** | | | | |
| Associated fields | - | Yes | - | - |
| Associated triggers | - | Yes | Yes | - |
| All Objects Referenced by this Object... | | Yes | Yes | - |
| All Objects referenced by this Object's fields... | - | Yes | - | - |
| **Modification allowed to:** | | | | |
| Object's sequence number | - | Yes | Yes | - |
| Object's name | No | Yes | Yes | Yes |
| Associated field names | - | - | - | Yes |
| Associated block name | - | - | - | Yes |
| (x, y) screen coordinate | - | - | Yes | - |
| Comment scroll region | - | Yes | Yes | Yes |

1 It is important to be extra-careful when modifying the name of a Block, Field, or Trigger that is itself referenced. It is possible to disrupt functionality by changing the name if it is directly referenced by another object (such as a Trigger or Form-Level Procedure), so generally: *Do not modify the name of a referenced block, field, trigger, or procedure after it has been referenced once or more.*

2 The designer is not allowed to modify any characteristics of the objects that are owned or referenced by the referenced Block or Field (Triggers and Procedures do not own anything: Steps in V2 Triggers are not specifically discussed in the Oracle literature on this subject, but one may assume that they are 'part of' the V2 Trigger for the purposes of this discussion). So generally, *do not modify any characteristic of a referenced block, field, or trigger after it has been referenced once or more.*

3 There is nothing wrong with modifying the screen position of a field that has been brought from a referenced field in another Form, but altering the coordinates of the referenced field may cause problems if there is code specifically relating to the field that requires it to appear at the same coordinates as it had before it was referenced.

**Hint**: if a wholly robust and local piece of code is required, it is probably better to *Copy the object* than to Reference it. The idea of a 'Library' of frequently copied elements is a good one.

# Practical Session Four

In the following practicals, try to be as efficient as possible in the way you work. It is a good idea to Save after every few Generate commands, rather than to keep Generating alone.

1 There is a consensus among end users in Parallel Universe Recruitment that 'error codes' should be straightforward and friendly, so your Project Manager has directed that you should arrange to capture SQL*Forms system output reports in the Message Line of the PERSON Form and replace them when they are produced in Block B1, thus:

*The following messages should be replaced:*
**`'Last row of query retrieved.'`** with:
`'REPORT: Sorry... no more people returned by your QUERY'`
**`'Query cancelled.'`** with:
`'REPORT: You have now left System QUERY MODE.'`
Any other message, with:
`'INFORMATION:'` and the message text itself.

The following errors should be replaced:
**`'At first record.'`** with:
`'REPORT: There is no one listed prior to this person.'`
Any other error with:
`'SORRY: ERROR!'` and the error text itself.

Any FATAL error should be replaced with:
`'Sorry! A serious problem, of TYPE nnnnn, has arisen! Please notify your DBA.'`, where nnnnn is the error code generated.

**Hint**: try not to make use of the Error Codes Book, or of the *SQL*Forms Designer's Reference*, so you will need to look *carefully* at what is actually going on in SQL*Forms, and you will need to remember what you have read! There are a couple of major hints in the phrasing of the question in any case: Remember, too, that the idea of the exercise is that you learn from it: it is not a test of ability, so you have exactly enough information to help you here.

2 The Manager of Parallel Universe Recruitment, Samantha Deridoes, has asked you to adjust the PERSON Form specially. She wants you to implement a choice of operation for the main screen personal data displayed. Her memo is as follows:

*I should be grateful if you could spare the time to make the following adjustments to the PERSON application. First, when a consultant's cursor is in the SNUM field only, the 'List Keys' screen (brought up with the [function keys] key?) should display a special key called 'Block Functionality', that will replace the PRINT key (someone said this was called KEY-PRINT, is that right?).*

*Second, if a consultant presses [block functionality], a little window should pop-up on screen, presenting a choice between 'Names Only' and 'Full Details' operation, using an arrow and the [return] key only.**

*Third, if 'Names Only' is chosen*, only the SNUM, SURNAME, FORENAME, SEX, BORN, AGE, NEXT_BIRTHDAY, and TODAY fields that we defined should be visible: all the others should vanish totally, and be unenterable.*

*Fourth, if 'Full Details' is chosen, all the screen fields should be visible and enterable.*

*Fifth, if the consultant presses any key other than [exit/cancel], the [up] key, or the [down] key or [next field] key, the cursor should simply return to SNUM as a safety measure, and the window should vanish.*

*Lastly, I have no requirement that the error trapping code you implemented for Dennis should operate in the window when it is running.*

*Do let me know how you get on.*

**Samantha Deridoes**

* Through telepathy, you perceive that Samantha means that the screen layout should appear as it does in Figs 6.2 and 6.3. Note that the operator must use the usual [up] and [down] keys to move the pointer arrow up and down, making it point to either option. As a quality assurance point, and because it looks better, you should arrange for the flashing cursor to appear in the field in which the arrow appears.

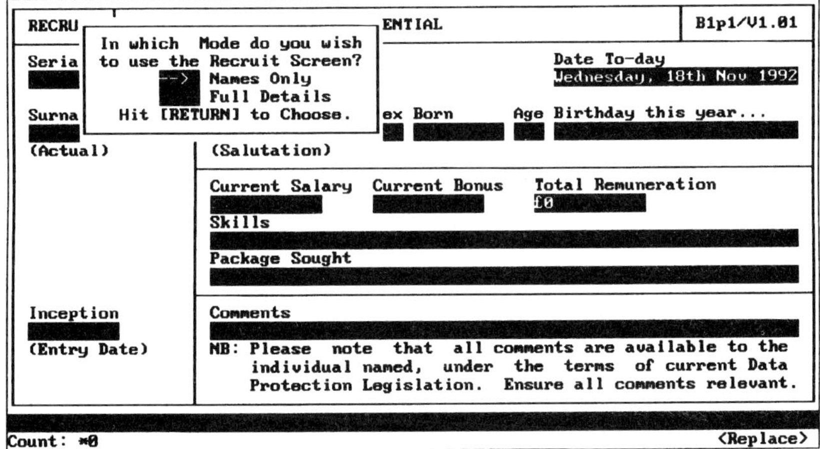


*Figure 6.2 Proposed layout for the 'Little Window'.*

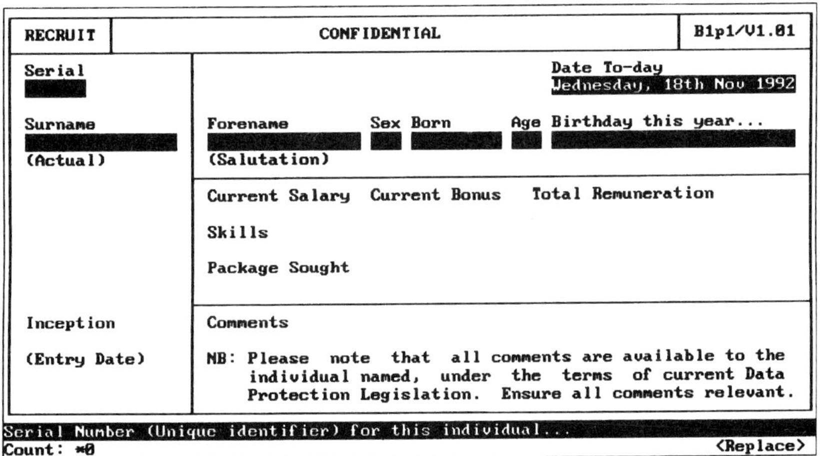


*Figure 6.3 Proposed appearance for 'Names Only'.*

# PART THREE

# APPENDICES: Data, additional information, addenda

*Cease, Man, to mourn, to weep, to wail;*
*Enjoy the shining hour of the Sun.*
*We dance along Death's icy brink,*
*But is the dance less full of fun?*

*From* The Kasidah

*Sir Richard Burton*

APPENDIX A

# DEFINITIONS FOR EXAMPLE WORK

## Table definitions for example work

This appendix details the definitions for the tables in the main text, using the standard output from the DESCRIBE command in SQL*Plus.

```
SQL> desc client
 Name                            Null?    Type
 ------------------------------- -------- ----
 CCODE                           NOT NULL NUMBER(4)
 SHORTNAME                       NOT NULL CHAR(25)
 ADDRESS1                                 CHAR(25)
 ADDRESS2                                 CHAR(25)
 ADDRESS3                                 CHAR(25)
 COUNTRY                                  CHAR(25)
 POSTCODE                                 CHAR(15)
 PHONE                                    CHAR(20)
 INCEP                                    DATE
 COMMENTS                                 LONG
```

**SQL> desc project**

```
 Name                            Null?    Type
 ------------------------------- -------- ----
 PCODE                           NOT NULL NUMBER(4)
 CCODE                           NOT NULL NUMBER(4)
 PNAME                           NOT NULL CHAR(15)
 TOTBUDGET                                NUMBER(10)
 STARTDATE                                DATE
 ENDDATE                                  DATE
```

**SQL> desc assignment**

```
 Name                            Null?    Type
 ------------------------------- -------- ----
 PCODE                           NOT NULL NUMBER(4)
 ACODE                           NOT NULL NUMBER(4)
 SNUM                            NOT NULL NUMBER(4)
 PJOBTITLE                                CHAR(15)
 QUOTEDPRICE                              NUMBER(9,2)
```

**SQL> desc recruit**

```
 Name                            Null?    Type
 ------------------------------- -------- ----
 SNUM                            NOT NULL NUMBER(4)
 SURNAME                         NOT NULL CHAR(15)
 FORENAME                                 CHAR(15)
 BORN                                     DATE
 SEX                                      CHAR(1)
 CURSAL                                   NUMBER(9,2)
 BONUS                                    NUMBER(9,2)
 SKILLCOM                                 CHAR(255)
 PACKAGE                                  CHAR(255)
 INCEP                                    DATE
 COMMENTS                                 LONG
```

# Data definitions for example tables

### Table A.1 Recruit

| *SNUM* | Surname | Forename | Born | Sex | Cursal | Bonus |
|---|---|---|---|---|---|---|
| 4001 | Shackle | Matthew | 28-Aug-60 | M | 16300 | 0 |
| 4002 | Gartner | Richard | 14-Feb-66 | M | 23420 | 1250 |
| 4003 | Raja | Saad | 21-Nov-63 | M | 21500 | 860 |
| 4004 | Chan | Chun Hoi | 02-Apr-57 | M | 34765 | 0 |
| 4005 | King | Helen | 14-Jun-70 | F | 18420 | 750 |
| 4006 | Bate | Susan | 16-May-60 | F | 28600 | 1200 |
| 4007 | Macrae | Clare | 13-Dec-65 | F | 22000 | 1200 |
| 4008 | Kumar | John | 27-Sep-59 | M | 32200 | 0 |
| 4009 | Brock | Margaret | 13-Jun-54 | F | 24800 | 2340 |

*Table continues thus horizontally...*

| *SNUM* | SKILLCOM |
|---|---|
| *4001* | Fortran, Z80 Assembler, RPGIII |
| *4002* | C, C++, BASIC, COBOL, ORACLE, DFDs, JSD, JSP, Project Management |
| *4003* | COBOL, C, FOCUS, DB2(rusty) |
| *4004* | Oracle SQL*Forms, PL/SQL, SQL*Plus, SQL, Pro*C, SSADM |
| *4005* | C, Oracle SQL, SQL*Plus |
| *4006* | Algol, COBOL, PL/1, Ada, C++, Ingres |
| *4007* | Project Management, Business Analysis, SSADM, CASE*Method |
| *4008* | Novell, DOS 5, Unix, Ultrix, C++, INFORMIX, DB2, COBOL |
| *4009* | CAD/CAM, Project Management, Merise, SSA, Data Modelling |

*Table continues thus horizontally...*

| *SNUM* | PACKAGE |
|---|---|
| *4001* | 18500 + pension + car |
| *4002* | 26000 + healthplan + mortgage |
| *4003* | 24000 + pension + car |
| *4004* | 38000 + pension + healthplan + car + company credit card |
| *4005* | 20000 + pension |
| *4006* | 30000 + car + pension + mortgage |
| *4007* | 25000 + car + personal mileage |
| *4008* | 38500 + relocation grant + mortgage + pension |
| *4009* | 27000 + pension |

*Table continues thus horizontally...*

| ***SNUM*** | **INCEP** | **COMMENTS** |
|---|---|---|
| *4001* | 12-Aug-92 | |
| *4002* | 01-May-92 | |
| *4003* | 20-Dec-91 | |
| *4004* | 07-Sep-92 | |
| *4005* | 07-Sep-92 | |
| *4006* | 15-Apr-92 | |
| *4007* | 20-May-92 | |
| *4008* | 04-Oct-92 | |
| *4009* | 13-Jul-92 | |

## Table A2: Client

| ***CCODE*** | **SHORTNAME** | **ADDRESS1** | **ADDRESS2** |
|---|---|---|---|
| 5114 | Descartes Ltd | 7 - 8 Shirley Drive | Hove |
| 5116 | Wittgenstein GMBH | Scheinerstrasse 2 | D-8000 Muenchen 80 |
| 5117 | Ghazali Textiles Ltd | Bastwick Street | London |
| 5221 | Vaager Life | Sondre Kongsvei 2 | Begby |
| 5222 | Nybble Consulting | 59 Brighton Road | Redhill |
| 5223 | Similarity UK Ltd | Narbury Court | 24 - 31 London Road |
| 5224 | United Snake Oils Ltd | 294 - 300 Abingdon Road | Headington |

*Table continues thus horizontally...*

| ***CCODE*** | **ADDRESS3** | **COUNTRY** | **POSTCODE** | **PHONE** |
|---|---|---|---|---|
| *5114* | Sussex | UK | BN3 8SP | 0273 417198 |
| *5116* | | Germany | | +89 922 18432 |
| *5117* | | UK | EC1V 3PE | 071 251 4961 |
| *5221* | 1630 Gamle Fredrikstad | Norway | | +09 346259 |
| *5222* | Surrey | UK | RH1 8YL | 0737 766888 |
| *5223* | Newbury, BERKSHIRE | UK | RG13 2JZ | 0635 528599 |
| *5224* | Oxford | UK | OX3 9HL | 0865 741727 |

*Table continues thus horizontally...*

| ***CCODE*** | **INCEP** | **COMMENTS** |
|---|---|---|
| *5114* | 16-Mar-92 | |
| *5116* | 03-Apr-92 | |
| *5117* | 27-Jun-92 | |
| *5221* | 15-Nov-91 | |
| *5222* | 18-Aug-92 | |
| *5223* | 18-Dec-91 | |
| *5224* | 19-Sep-92 | |

# APPENDIX B

# USING PL/SQL DML COMMANDS

This appendix discusses the use of DML commands in PL/SQL. These were not covered in the text because the book is orientated purely towards SQL*Forms, which performs its own retrieval, updating, and deletion operations using internally generated DML. DML commands, are, of course, INSERT, UPDATE, and DELETE. The SELECT command is traditionally included in the list because it does literally manipulate data, though they will not be changed by it unless SELECT is used in combination with one of the other three commands.

## Program output: INSERT and assignment

INSERT INTO *table* ($col_1$, ... , $col_n$) VALUES ($val_1$, ... , $val_n$);
*:BLOCKNAME.fieldname* := *PL/SQL_variable*;

PL/SQL is primarily a transaction processing language. Therefore it will not allow the printout or display of data from within programs written in it. There is no PRINT statement. If there are any data that need simply to be printed, then these must be stored in tables in the database with which the program code is associated. Alternatively, the PRINT command in a host language may be used, where PL/SQL is operated in conjunction with a pre-compiler and embedded. In

SQL*Forms, naturally, output can be sent either to the database or to screen fields.

INSERT functions exactly as the standard SQL DML command. Note that it is entirely permissible to place functions and evaluated expressions within the VALUES clause.

Where output to a screen field is required, simple assignment using the := operator is used. *There is no need for SELECT ... INTO!* For example:

```
DECLARE
   A1    NUMBER    := 12345;
   B1    NUMBER    := 5678;
   C1    CHAR(10)  := 'VIEHOFF';
   D1    NUMBER    := 1500;
BEGIN
   INSERT INTO RECRUIT
   (SNUM, INCEP, CURSAL, SURNAME)
   VALUES (3333, '12-aug-92',
           A1 + B1 + (1.15 * D1), INITCAP(C1));
   :b1.sal_field := A1 + B1 + (1.15 * D1);
   :b1.sur_field := INITCAP(C1);
   :b1.incep := '12-aug-92';
END;
```

## Program output INSERT —and assignment rules—

- Date and character data must always be enclosed in single quotes.
- Individual clauses in VALUES must be separated by commas.
- VALUES are always inserted into a table's columns from the left-hand side (first CREATEd column), unless otherwise specified in brackets after the name of the table.
- The table into which VALUES are placed must already exist, and the current user must have INSERT privileges.
- Columns omitted from the name list will take a NULL value for the currently inserted row.

- Screen fields and the blocks to which they belong *must exist* before the code is compiled in the trigger step where they are referenced, otherwise an error will result!
- Obviously, it must be possible for values to be placed into the block fields specified. The operator does not have to be able to enter them or see them, though.

# Program output: using UPDATE

UPDATE *table* SET $col_1$ = $expr_1$, ... , $col_n$ = $expr_n$ WHERE *condition*;

UPDATE is much the same in relation to PL/SQL as it is for standard SQL. It is used to change existing values stored in tables by setting a column to an expression, *<expr>*. *No rules are listed here, because UPDATE follows the standard SQL syntax and construction rules.*

### Example 1: Normal usage

Note that any variable names used in the DECLARE section *must be unique* within the program as a whole so that they may be differentiated from any table's columns.

```
DECLARE
  PERC_ADJ   NUMBER := 1.15;
  SAL_ADJ    NUMBER := 1.12;
  DN         NUMBER := 9006;
BEGIN
  UPDATE     RECRUIT
  SET        CURSAL = CURSAL * SAL_ADJ,
             BONUS = BONUS * PERC_ADJ
  WHERE      SNUM = DN;
END;
```

### Example 2: Using a subquery

In the example below, column aliases have been used merely to show that they are available: they are not essential to the operation of the program here. *Note that the subquery should only return one row, otherwise the UPDATE will fail: there is no allowance in SQL for obtaining more than one row in a SET clause.*

```
DECLARE
   PERC_ADJ    NUMBER := 1.15;
   SAL_ADJ     NUMBER := 1.12;
   SN          NUMBER(4) := 9006;
BEGIN
   UPDATE   RECRUIT R
   SET(R.CURSAL, R.BONUS)=
           (SELECT  X.CURSAL * SAL_ADJ,
                    X.BONUS * PERC_ADJ
            FROM    RECRUIT X
            WHERE   X.SNUM = 3788)
   WHERE R.SURNAME = :b1.surname
   AND   R.SNUM    = SN;
END;
```

The layout and aliasing used within the program is not essential, but it improves speed and readability and therefore ease of debugging very considerably.

# Program output: using DELETE

DELETE FROM *table* WHERE *condition*;

DELETE is much the same in relation to PL/SQL as it is for standard SQL. It is used to delete existing rows stored in tables, either removing all of them or merely a selection using the WHERE clause's *<condition>. No rules are listed here, because DELETE follows the standard SQL syntax and construction rules.* Two examples follow.

### Example 1: Normal DELETE

Note that any variable names used in the DECLARE section *must be unique* within the program as a whole so that they may be differentiated from any table's columns.

```
DECLARE
    IN_DT     NUMBER := '12-JUN-89';
BEGIN
    DELETE  FROM RECRUIT
    WHERE   INCEP = IN_DT;
END;
```

### Example 2: Using a subquery

Here, a subquery may return more than one row, providing that a suitable operator such as IN( ) is used.

```
DECLARE
    MIL_MAX     NUMBER := 20000;
BEGIN
    DELETE  FROM RECRUIT R
    WHERE R.SNUM IN
            (SELECT A.SNUM
             FROM   ASSIGNMENT A
             WHERE  A.QUOTEDPRICE >= MIL_MAX);
END;
```

# Transactions: COMMIT and ROLLBACK

COMMIT [WORK];
ROLLBACK [WORK];

Whenever a database command (DDL or DML) is issued within ORACLE, the user has the option to COMMIT or ROLLBACK the series of operations performed by the system. It is helpful to restate the rules that apply to standard COMMIT and ROLLBACK functions here. A series of operations is known as a TRANSACTION (or 'Commit Unit'), and has been defined by Oracle Corporation as

> 'The group of events that occur between one time and the next time that a user connects to ORACLE, disconnects from ORACLE, commits changes to the database, or rolls changes back.'

Therefore a COMMIT will effectively store the changes specified by the user in UPDATE, INSERT, and other commands, making them permanent. However, a ROLLBACK will reverse the changes, preventing them from permanently altering the database. Data can therefore be thought of as sitting in a 'buffer' or store, until a COMMIT (to store it) or a ROLLBACK (to cancel it) is issued.

Before changes are committed, they will appear to have altered the database, and subsequent retrieval or other commands will act as though the changes have taken place. Other users of the ORACLE system will *not* see them, however.

Once COMMIT has been parsed, all changes since the last COMMIT (the end of the last transaction) will become permanent, and will be visible to other users querying (or operating upon) the tables within which the changes have taken place, provided that they have the appropriate authority to view the data. ROLLBACK can therefore be used to correct errors caused by the use of Data Manipulation Language commands.

Entering the command COMMIT yields no report other than 'commit complete'. Entering ROLLBACK yields no report other than 'rollback complete'. The word WORK is optional, and is included from ANSI compatibility.

COMMIT and ROLLBACK may be included at any appropriate point in a PL/SQL program where the designer is certain that one or the other function must be performed.

## Transactions: using SAVEPOINTS

SAVEPOINT *savepoint_name*;
ROLLBACK [WORK] TO *savepoint_name*;

Introduced in Version 6, a SAVEPOINT is a *named point in time in a transaction (commit-unit)*. If several commands take place in a transaction it can be useful to be able to reverse a selection rather than all of them. SAVEPOINTs are therefore used in conjunction with ROLLBACK to allow a portion of the transaction to be rolled back. A SAVEPOINT may have any name, up to 30 characters, provided that it is unique within the transaction in which it occurs. There may be a maximum of five SAVEPOINTs per transaction, by default. The DBA may change this to allow a total of 255 for that instance of Oracle. Once a transaction has been COMMITted or rolled back as a whole, all the named SAVEPOINTs are deleted.

In order to make use of a SAVEPOINT, the operator types the command at the SQL prompt (or places it within a SQL*Plus batch file) together with its name. The name then serves as a label for this point in time. If there is a need to reverse a portion of the transaction, the operator merely types ROLLBACK TO and the name of the SAVEPOINT back to which the transaction should be rolled. This has the effect of performing a ROLLBACK upon all DML functions that have been performed (in this transaction) beyond that point in time. Preceding SAVEPOINTs will remain in effect, thus a ROLLBACK WORK TO may be performed to the same savepoint several times. Both this savepoint and all those preceding it will vanish as soon as a COMMIT or ROLLBACK is actuated. For example:

```
SAVEPOINT swallow;

UPDATE command...;
UPDATE command...;
INSERT command...;
INSERT command...;

SAVEPOINT reed_warbler;

DELETE command...;
DELETE command...;

SAVEPOINT heron;

INSERT command...;

ROLLBACK WORK TO reed_warbler;
```

This will ROLLBACK all the DML between reed_warbler and the ROLLBACK command. When the user types COMMIT or ROLLBACK, the transaction will be COMMITed or rolled back, and all the SAVEPOINTs will vanish. SAVEPOINTs are ideally used where there are conditional and branching commands, covered in Chapter 2.

# Example: program using COMMIT

The following program incidentally combines a selection of the preceding DML command examples, and includes COMMIT and SAVEPOINT to show a possible scenario. *Obviously, additional logic would need to be coded to enable ROLLBACK TO a named SAVEPOINT based upon a defined condition test—this is omitted for simplicity.*

Note how the designer has named the SAVEPOINTs carefully to indicate precisely before which event they occur. Each SAVEPOINT has also been assigned here a sequential number, 01, to allow for similarly named SAVEPOINTs in a larger version of the program. Remember that, by default there may be a maximum of five SAVEPOINTS per transaction.

```
DECLARE
    A1          NUMBER := 12345;
    B1          NUMBER := 5678;
    C1          CHAR(10) := 'VIEHOFF';
    D1          NUMBER := 1500;
    MIL_MAX     NUMBER := 20000;
    SN          NUMBER(4) := 3107;
    PERC_ADJ    NUMBER := 1.15;
    SAL_ADJ     NUMBER := 1.12;
    DN          NUMBER := 20;
BEGIN
    /* This program assumes a personnel system, *
     * system based around a non-base table     *
     * called STAFF, containing people's        *
     * salaries, surnames, and so forth.        */
    LOCK TABLE STAFF IN ROW SHARE MODE;
    SAVEPOINT PRE_DELETE_01;
    DELETE FROM STAFF  S
    WHERE  S.SNUM IN
               (SELECT   V.SNUM
                FROM     VEHICLE V
                WHERE    V.MILEAGE > MIL_MAX);
```

```
    SAVEPOINT PRE_UPDATE_01;
    UPDATE   STAFF S
    SET      (S.SALARY, S.BONUS)=
             (SELECT    X.SALARY * SAL_ADJ,
                        X.BONUS * PERC_ADJ
              FROM      STAFF X
              WHERE     X.SNUM = 3788)
    WHERE    S.DIV = DN
    AND      S.SNUM = SN;
    SAVEPOINT PRE_INSERT_01;
    INSERT INTO STAFF
    (SNUM, DIV, SALARY, SURNAME)
    VALUES (3333,  20,  A1 + B1 + (1.15 * D1),
          INITCAP(C1));
    COMMIT WORK;
END;
```

## APPENDIX C

# FORMATTING USING TO_CHAR( )

TO_CHAR(*date*, 'date_picture')
TO_CHAR(*column*, 'numeric_picture')

This function will convert the <*date*> specified into a given format, <date picture>. There is a wide range of different formats, and these are given below. Note that capitalization is significant, so that 'DAY' will yield the name of the day in CAPITALS, while 'Day' will yield the first letter of the day in capitals. See Tables C.1 and C.2 for a full list of Date Formats, suffixes, and the fm prefix.

The TO_CHAR( ) function will also accept all the common SQL*Plus numeric formatting characters, using one 9 character to represent a single digit. For example:

```
SELECT TO CHAR(SYSDATE, 'fmDAY, ddth Month YYYY')
FROM   DUAL;

TO CHAR(SYSDATE,'FMDAY,DDTHMONTHYYYY')
-----------------------------------------------------
WEDNESDAY, 28th March 1990
```

**Table C1 Date formats available using TO_CHAR( )**

| Format | Meaning |
|---|---|
| / , . : ; | Include punctuation in output |
| *'text'* | <*text*> is included in the printed result |
| AD or A.D. | Millennium indicator (or with full stops) |
| AM or A.M. | Meridian indicator (or with full stops) |
| BC or B.C. | Millennium indicator (or with full stops) |
| C | Century |
| D | Day of the week |
| DD | Day of the month |
| DDD | Day of the year |
| DAY | Name of the day—capitals are significant |
| DY | 3-letter abbreviated day |
| HH or HH12 | 12-hour clock daily time |
| HH24 | 24-hour clock daily time |
| J | Julian day (stated since 1 January 4712 BC) |
| MM | Two-digit month |
| MON | Three-letter abbreviated month |
| MONTH | Full name of the month (capitals are significant) |
| MI | Minute |
| PM or P.M. | Meridian indicator (or with full stops) |
| Q | Quarter of the year |
| SS | Second |
| SSSSS | Seconds past midnight (zero to 86 399) |
| SCC | Century, prefixed with a hyphen if BC |
| SYEAR | Year spelled out in full (with hyphen if BC) |
| W or WW | Week of the year or month |
| Y | Last digit of the year |
| YY | Last two digits of the year |
| YYY | Last three digits of the year |
| Y,YYY | Year with comma placed |
| YEAR | Year spelled out in full text |

# Dates: prefixes and suffixes

fm

TH

SP

SPTH

There are a number of suffixes and one prefix that may be added to the characters specified in the date format. The prefix 'fm' in the format stands for 'fill mode'. When prefixing the characters, MONTH or DAY, blank padding will be suppressed, and the output date will be of variable length. The meanings of the suffixes are given in Table C.2.

**Table C.2 Suffix meanings**

| Suffix | Meaning | Example | Output |
|---|---|---|---|
| TH | Ordinal number | ddth | 4th |
| | | ddth | 3rd |
| | | ddth | 1st |
| SP | Spelled-out number | ddsp | four |
| | | ddsp | twenty-three |
| | | ddsp | one |
| SPTH | Spelled-out ordinal numbers | ddspth | fourth |
| | | ddspth | twenty-third |
| | | ddspth | first |

## Including text in date strings

Where the user needs to include words like 'of' or 'the', these should be included in the date format but enclosed in double quotes to prevent ORACLE from interpreting the text as an (erroneous) date format: For example:

```
to_char(joindate, 'fmDay, ''the'' ddth ''of'' Month
YYYY')
```

APPENDIX D

# EXAMPLE PAGE ATTRIBUTES' ADJUSTMENTS

For the following examples the PERSON Form was used in its Default layout. There were two Blocks, B1 (based on the RECRUIT table) and B2 (also based upon RECRUIT). All columns were used for each Block. B1 was positioned on Page 1; B2 on Page 2, to which all the attribute changes were applied.

1 B2's Page 2 coordinates were initially set as in Fig. D.1 with the effect when, at runtime, the operator moves into Block B2 (Fig. D.2). Note how the pop-

```
 Action  foRm  Block  Field  Trigger  Procedure  Image  Help  Options
                              Page Definition

   Page Number: 2                       [ X ] Pop Up

   Page Size: X:        Y:              [ X ] Border
   View Size: X: 35     Y: 15           [   ] Vertical Scroll Bar
   View Loc:  X: 40     Y: 15           [   ] Horizontal Scroll Bar
   View Page: X: 40     Y: 15           [ X ] Remove on Exit

   Title: B2 View Page @(40, 15)

Enter the title for the page.  It will appear on the window.
Frm: PERSON        Blk: b2          Fld:             Trg:              <Rep>
```

*Figure D.1   B2's Page 2 coordinates.*

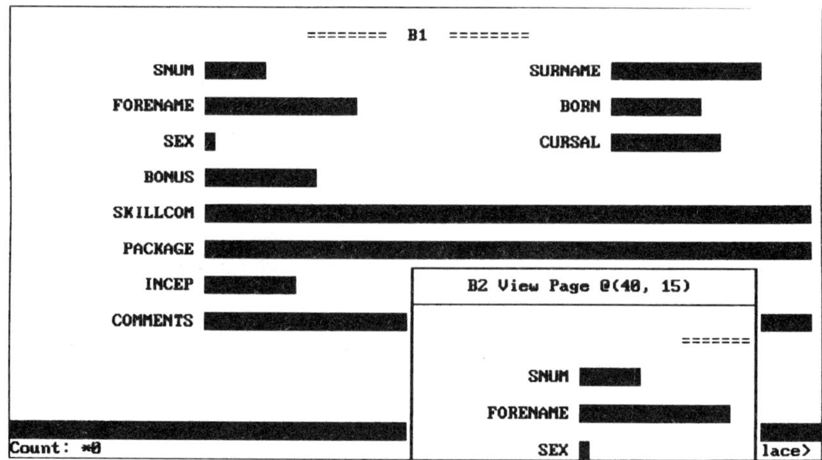


*Figure D.2 Block B2.*

up is too long for the screen (height 15 rows), so it spills over. In a bitmapped GUI system the operator could resize the window to see the rest.

2 B2's Page 2 View Location coordinates are changed to (10, 10), so that the whole view fits on to the screen and pops-up correctly over Page 1 (Fig. D.3).

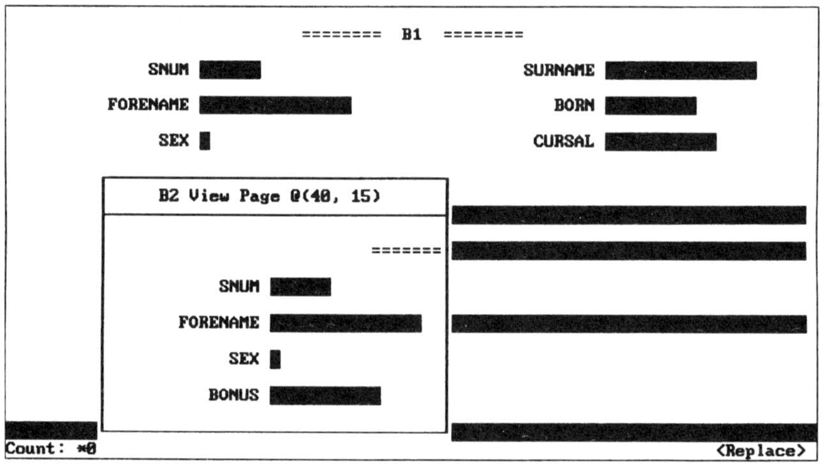


*Figure D.3 B2's Page 2 View Location coordinates.*

3 B2's View Page coordinates are changed to (15, 4) (Fig. D.4).

4 Finally, B2's Page 2 View Size coordinates are changed to (3, 15): the cursor is still flashing on SNUM (Fig. D.5)!

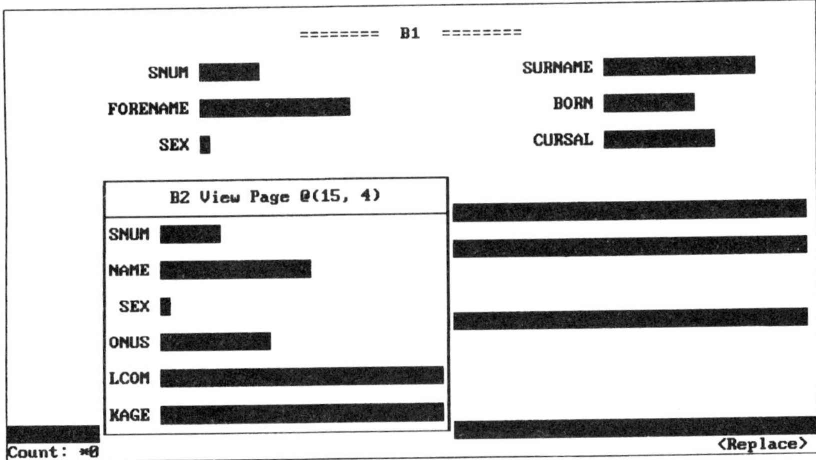


*Figure D.4* *B2's View Page coordinates.*

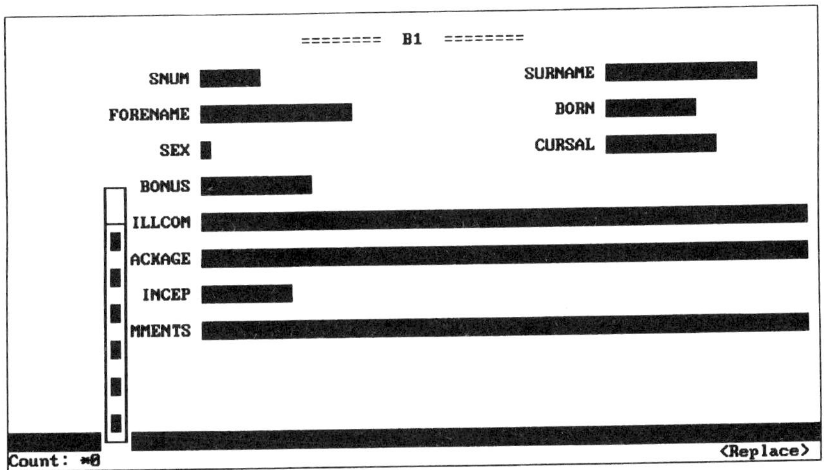


*Figure D.5* *B2's Page View Size coordinates.*

It is important to remember that if a field has a 'Required' attribute, or if the sequence of fields in the Block requires it, Forms appears to force the View Page to show the field regardless of any additional setting the designer has made. Hence, despite altering a View Page, there may be no perceptible change in operation. Effective attribute adjustment, therefore, must be made in conjunction with more general functionality design. These considerations, to some extent, will be simpler in the case of window-based GUI applications due to the ease of resizing and view alteration by the operator at runtime.

# GLOSSARY

*340. One cannot guess how a word functions.*
*One has to* **look at** *its use and learn from that.*
*But the difficulty is to remove the prejudice which*
*stands in the way of doing this. It is not a* **stupid** *prejudice.*

***Proposition 340 from*** **Philosophical Investigations, Part 1**

*Ludwig Wittgenstein*

Note that where given, the Oracle technical terms used in this glossary relate to Oracle SQL*Forms Version 3.0 and Kernel Version 6.0. Many terms are the same in Kernel Version 7.0, but SQL*Forms Version 4.0 has additions and changes. Some of the terms given are those used in this book for convenience and are not necessarily standard.

**3GL** – Third Generation Language. Generally, a procedural, often English-like programming language. Traditional examples include COBOL, Fortran, and BASIC. More sophisticated examples include C and Lisp. A 3GL is usually characterized by the idea of the programmer telling the computer exactly how to work at every stage of operation, so a 3GL is classically a 'how to'-orientated language. 3GLs usually contain iterative, recursive, directive, and conditional constructs.

**4GL** – Fourth Generation Language. The most advanced commercially available type of programming language. Often English-like, 4GLs are usually associated with tools such as databases. They represent the highest stage of language development because they automatically deal with low-level storage and retrieval mechanisms, and often simple data formatting, without the intervention or structuring of the programmer. Examples include SQL, Prolog, SQL*Forms, and, latterly, screen-based front-end tools such as those provided by Gupta's SQLWindows™ and Microsoft Access™, as well as sophisticated word processors and spreadsheets. 4GLs are considered to be 'What To'-orientated languages, because the programmer can rely on a range of facilities already dealt with automatically, and needs merely to specify what information is required and from where, rather than how to obtain it. 4GLs often lack the need for program control in the classical sense, since their primary aim is usually to answer questions or define or manipulate a storage mechanism.

**Active set** – The set of zero, one, or many rows returned by the SELECT statement that constitutes an Explicit Cursor once that cursor has been explicitly opened using the OPEN verb.

**Anonymous Block** – A series of PL/SQL statements constituting a PL/SQL Block but lacking BEGIN and END keywords. Only legal within a SQL*Forms trigger or Form-Level Procedure.

**ASC** – Automatic Search and Complete. This procedure relates to List of Values operation. (See notes on the LIST_VALUES Packaged Procedure in Chapter 5.)

**Base Table** – The database table defined by the designer as relating to one or more Blocks in a SQL*Forms application.

**Block (1)** – or 'PL/SQL block': a series of one or more PL/SQL statements, usually preceded by a BEGIN statement and terminated by an END statement. Each statement will be terminated with a semi-colon. Optionally, the Block may include a DECLARE section for initializing variables, and an EXCEPTION section for including exception-handling code statements.

**Block (2)** – The fundamental SQL*Forms building unit, with a name of up to 30 characters. A Block acts as the SQL*Forms equivalent of a database table, holding data returned from a Base Table to which it relates in the database. There may be a minimum of one Block in a Form. A Block may have a maximum of one Base Table; a minimum of zero Base Tables. A Block normally owns one or more Fields that will contain the data, and may own one or more triggers of different names.

**Block (3)** – A set of contiguous byte data stored on Winchester disk or flexible media. Blocks may be 'Physical', in which case they are controlled by the operating system, or 'Logical', in which case, although data will physically be stored in operating system-maintained blocks, the software controlling storage will treat data as though they were contained in notional blocks for the purpose of programmed operation. Oracle uses logical blocks to maintain B-Tree structured data in its Data Files, and a certain number will be allocated for each table.

**Block Mode** – A hardware operation mode in which semi-intelligent terminals which control character editing locally send data to the central processing unit in chunks or Blocks of data, terminated by one or more control characters. Usually this type of hardware is used across wide-area networks or with very large numbers of users to minimize cpu contention. It can prove problematic with modern versions of SQL*Forms due to the way designers require triggers to actuate during navigation. Usually, such problems can be minimized by implementing triggers based around Function Keys ('PF Keys'), since these normally send an immediate code to the cpu, allowing the trigger to actuate. Validation issues can also cause problems, and the scope of validation in SQL*Forms can be adjusted by altering the 'Validation Unit' setting. (See also **Character Mode**.)

**Blue Wardrobe** – An old name for an IBM mainframe hardware system module, since it was IBM Blue in colour and the chassis had a door at the front for access.

**Boolean** – The datatype associated with the ideas of George Boole (1815 – 1864), who defined the concept of 1 as representing TRUTH and 0 as representing FALSITY, therefore the bi-state mathematical truth representation used in Boolean algebra. In Oracle PL/SQL, Booleans are effectively tri-state variables, since they may take the states TRUE, FALSE, or NULL.

**Cha-Cha** – The informal name for the error that occurs if you TO_CHAR a CHAR datatype. Oracle cannot turn a character into a character in PL/SQL! The associated type of error usually occurs in relation to the MESSAGE packaged procedure when concatenating a variable with a piece of literal text.

**Character Mode** – The most common SQL*Forms operating mode, the term refers to the type of terminal and central processing unit hardware configuration whereby the cpu continuously monitors the operator's keyboard (or monitors for the defined timeslice on a multi-process system.) Each character is monitored by the cpu, hence the name of the mode. The mode allows any triggers to be fired in the correct event sequence, since navigation will operate in the normal manner without any constraint upon the scope of trigger firing as there may be in Block Mode. (See also **Block Mode**.)

**Check Box** – SQL*Forms(Design) or SQL*Forms(Run Form) runtime field that may take an 'X' character or a space value. Its completion with an 'X' indicates that the attribute or functionality to which it relates will be actuated; its completion with a space indicates that the attribute or functionality will not be actuated.

**Commit Unit** – Also known as a 'Transaction': the group of events that occur between one time and the next time that a user connects to Oracle, disconnects from Oracle, commits changes to the database, or rolls changes back.

**Compiler** – Traditionally, a software mechanism that converts symbolic source program code into binary object machine code. The term latterly means any type of mechanism that converts symbolic (usually, English-like) source code into a type of object code that can be read and actuated by another software mechanism at a faster speed. Usually, modern compilers assist the developer by producing error messages and commented erroneous program code. The PL/SQL compiler in SQL*Forms converts SQL and PL/SQL statements into runtime code prior to application execution.

**Conditional** – A program clause or verb construct that tests for logical truth in a mathematical or algebraic formula, function, or attribute. In PL/SQL, keywords such as IF and EXIT represent conditionals.

**Constant** – A literal that remains set throughout a known runtime period, either in relation to the whole or part of an executing program. Alternatively, a variable that remains set to its instantiated value throughout a known runtime period.

**Control Block** – A SQL*Forms block that maps to zero base tables in the database. Usually used as a logical owner structure for processing field contents or for owning trigger code in a SQL*Forms application. Also known as NBI-Block.

**Cursor (1)** – An area in random access memory also known as a 'Context Area' that contains all the information necessary to parse a Structured Query Language command. A Cursor will be opened implicitly (automatically) by Oracle whenever the statement parser encounters a piece of SQL. Also known as an '**implicit Cursor**.'

**Cursor (2)** – A named area in random access memory opened by the programmer's code that will contain all the information necessary to parse a Structured Query Language command in SQL or Embedded Structured Query

Language (ESQL) or PL/SQL. This type of cursor will be prefixed by the keyword CURSOR in a declarative program section and its SQL parsed by the verb OPEN. Also known as an '**explicit Cursor**.'

**Cursor (3)** – A flashing bar or block character that represents the current position of the operator's text typing marker on the VDU.

**Cursor (4)** – A visible external marker object that indicates the current field in a running SQL*Forms application. A cursor may have two states: 'Outside Form' and 'Field Instance'. (See also **Navigation Unit**.)

**DDL** – Data Definition Language. This is the Structured Query Language sublanguage that contains the commands that create and adjust structures in Oracle. There are only three commands in ISO/ANSI standard SQL: CREATE, ALTER, and DROP. In Oracle there may be many different objects to which these commands can relate. Examples include Tables, Clusters, Indexes, Tablespaces, Synonyms, Views, Sequences, and Triggers in Oracle7.

**Dialogue (or 'Dialog') Box** – Pop-up window appearing during SQL*Forms(Run Form) or SQL*Forms(Design) runtime, having at least one field into which the operating user may type text.

**Directive** – A program verb construct that forces program control to act in a known way. In PL/SQL, commands such as GOTO and RAISE represent directives.

**DML** – Data Manipulation Language. This is the Structured Query Language sublanguage that contains the commands that adjust table data themselves. There are only three commands in ISO/ANSI standard SQL: INSERT, UPDATE, and DELETE. Although it cannot affect data by itself since it is a reporting tool, the SELECT verb can be used in combination with each of the three DML commands, so it is normally regarded as part of DML. This also applies to the SELECT ... INTO construct, though it is illegal in cursors in PL/SQL and cannot be used in combination with any INSERT, UPDATE, or DELETE command.

**Dongle** – Small PC hardware security device, often hanging from a spare system port and preventing system operation by unauthorized users.

**DUAL** – A dummy table in Oracle containing the single value 'X' in a column called DUMMY. Although, traditionally owned by the user SYSTEM (so fully specified as SYSTEM.DUAL) from Oracle Kernel Version 6.0, DUAL has been owned by the user SYS, although the older synonym has been retained for version compatibility.

**Exception** – Any pre-defined or designer-defined occurrence during the runtime of a PL/SQL Block. Exceptions are named and initialized in the declaration section of the block to which they belong, then they may be 'raised' during runtime. An Exception is simply a name for a program subpart. (See also **Raise** and **Propagation (Exceptions)**.)

**Exception Handler** – Program code contained in the optional EXCEPTION section of a PL/SQL Block, written by the programmer. Exception Handlers will begin execution when the named exception is 'raised' (invoked) during runtime. Control is passed to the Exception Handler in much the same way as it would be with a directive statement in a more traditional language. Exception Handlers are normally written in order to recover from unusual occurrences, errors, or perform special clear-up routines. They should not be written to perform everyday activities. (See also **Exception**, **Raise**, and **Propagation (Exceptions)**.)

**Explicit Cursor** – A cursor named by the programmer. (See also **Cursor (2)**.)

**Failure** – A technical SQL*Forms term, defined as a status normally occurring in a V2-Style trigger when one of the following occurs: (1) an SQL DML statement fails to act upon one or more table rows; (2) a trigger step cannot be executed for any reason; (3) a V2-Style Macro cannot be executed for any reason. (See also **Success** and **Step**.)

**Fatal Error** – A technical SQL*Forms term, defined as occurring when a command executed in a running SQL*Forms application causes the host operating system to run out of available memory for the operation.

**Field (1)** – The SQL*Forms version of a Table's column, with a name of up to 30 characters. In straightforward use, a field takes exactly the same name as the column in the Block's Base table from which its data come. Fields are physically owned by SQL*Forms Blocks, and may themselves own zero or more triggers of type V2 or type V3 construction. Additionally, fields have a large range of different attributes relating to their runtime operation. Form Fields are fields that have no direct connection to columns in a Block's Base Table.

**Field (2)** – A constituent of a PL/SQL record (outside the scope of this book), with a name of up to 30 characters. Fields may be referenced individually within a PL/SQL record by specifying them in the form RECORD.fieldname. For example, RECRUIT.surname.

**Form (1)** – An application developed in SQL*Forms and owning a minimum of one Block object. A Form owns Blocks, Pages, Form-Level Procedures, and Triggers.

**Form (2)** – A type of display layout for screens in SQL*Forms(Design), in which a full screen displays the relevant information for a SQL*Forms object, or in which other types of data might be displayed.

**Form-Level Function** – A SQL*Forms object designed to return a value to a calling PL/SQL trigger or Form-Level Procedure in SQL*Forms. These are implemented by the designer in the same way as Form-Level Procedures. They are not included within this scope of this book.

**Form-Level Procedure** – A non-event-related PL/SQL subprogram object, owned at Form Level by a SQL*Forms application. Form-Level Procedures must be invoked from a trigger at some point in the owning Form in order to operate. They can return values to or take values from a calling trigger through the use of one or more datatyped parameters. Form-Level Procedure syntax will be exactly the same as a normal PL/SQL trigger, but the very first PL/SQL Block may not include the keyword DECLARE if local variables are to be initialized.

**Global variable** – A SQL*Forms variable available throughout an application and transferable across applications within the same Forms runtime session. A Global variable may take a name of up to 30 characters, and must be prefixed with the word GLOBAL, in the form GLOBAL.variable_name. Global variables do not have to be declared, but they must be initialized by assigning a value to them.

**GUI** – Pronounced 'Gooey', a Graphical User Interface such as Microsoft Windows™, the Apple Macintosh™ graphical interface, and many others. GUIs are characterized by the use of windows, icons, mice, and pull-down menus, the combination known as 'wimps'.

**Implicit cursor** – A cursor opened automatically by Oracle itself. Implicit cursors always take the name 'SQL' when their attributes are referenced. (See also **Cursor (1)**.)

**Index variable** – A numeric integer variable implicitly declared as the loop control variable for a looping construct in PL/SQL. Its name may be up to 30 characters in length. If it must be referenced, an index variable can be identified by prefixing it with the name of the loop to which it belongs, providing that the loop itself is preceded by a label enclosed in wigwam symbols. Therefore an index variable could be referenced as LOOPNAME.index_variable. It is good practice not to change the value of an index variable by assignment during loop processing, though its value may be used in appropriate statements.

**Indirection** – Referencing the name of an object by referencing the name of an object containing that object's name as a literal. For example, in SQL*Forms, sending the Navigation Unit to the first enterable field of a block the name of which is stored in a field somewhere else. To effect this, the NAME_IN Packaged Function must be used in PL/SQL in SQL*Forms. Higher-level indirection can be performed by using parenthesized NAME_IN functions.

**Initialization** – Usually taken to mean the idea of 'setting a variable to a value or a NULL', initialization in fact refers to the process of defining a named memory area in random access memory that will be treated as a logical variable during the runtime of a PL/SQL program. Usually, the initialized variable will be instantiated just subsequent upon initialization.

**Instantiation** – In simple terms, setting a variable to a value.

**Label** – A designer-defined name for a subsection of a PL/SQL Block. Labels must prefix an executable statement, and may be up to 30 characters in length, enclosed by wigwam symbols. When referenced by GOTO or END-type statements, label names are not stated with wigwam symbols.

**List of Values** – A SQL*Forms facility whereby values are taken from a programmer-defined table column for display to the operator. In versions of SQL*Forms earlier than 3.0 there was only one version of a List of Values (sometimes called an an 'LOV'), which placed a single value into a block field, allowing the operator to tab through each of the retrieved items until an appropriate one was found, and leaving it in the field. From SQL*Forms Version 3.0, such a construct is known as a 'V2 List of Values'. Forms Version 3.0 enhances LOV functionality by allowing the programmer to specify a complete SQL query (either including or excluding the INTO keyword) which places one or more column values into a pop-up window that appears over the SQL*Forms page. These values may be scrolled-through by the operator, then a single value may be selected for insertion into the field. Note that advanced use allows more columns to be legally selected for display than are placed into the field, or many columns to be selected into many fields. This newer pop-up LOV is known as a 'V3 List of Values'.

**Lock** – An internal Oracle software mechanism that prevents more than one process at a time from physically adjusting a row or set of rows contained in a table, but allows more than one process to view one or more rows logically simultaneously. There are various different locking types that are more or less prohibitive in terms of access. Locks are otherwise of Implicit or Explicit type. Implicit Locks are taken out by Oracle itself; Explicit Locks are taken out by the programmer or other user, or user process, when they use the SQL statement LOCK..., of whatever type.

**Macro** – A SQL*Forms command often representing the same functionality as a pre-defined operator function keystroke, but extended to include directive and conditional constructs and additional facilities. Also known as 'V2 Macros', these commands can only be used in V2-Style Triggers. Macros are outside the scope of this book, but many of them are exactly the same as certain Packaged Procedures or their options.

**Navigation Unit** – An invisible internal marker object indicating the currently processing object in a runtime SQL*Forms application. The Navigation Unit has five states: 'Outside Form', 'Form', 'Block', 'Record', and 'Field Instance'. The current status of the Navigation Unit is contained in SQL*Forms System variables. (See also **Cursor (4)**.)

**Null** – Loosely defined as a known absence of anything, a null is literally an absent datum. It is not the same as zero or a space and it has no positive or negative assignment. Oracle Version 6.0 may physically store a null as zero or one bytes in length, depending upon the position of the column containing it within a table. Its use in PL/SQL, as with SQL, can yield to problems in algebraic expressions since they have a tendency to yield a null if associated with a constant or coefficient variable. The NVL function (in both SQL and PL/SQL) will return a known value in place of a null, if found, though the programmer should note that the value returned by NVL must be of the same datatype as the column or variable tested. Oracle7 stores nulls as zero bytes under all circumstances.

**OODBMS** – Object Oriented Database Management System. A database with a logical construction based around the idea of 'Objects'. At the time of writing, OODBMS are plagued by the lack of a general mathematical foundation such as that supporting the Relational model proposed by Ted Codd and forming the backbone of database systems such as DB2, Ingres, Oracle, Sybase, and others.

**Packaged Function** – A pre-defined SQL*Forms system function that will return a value to the calling PL/SQL statement, such as the last error message encountered or the presence of absence of a block or field attribute for a given block or field.

**Packaged Procedure** – A pre-defined SQL*Forms operation command, similar to a macro in older versions of SQL*Forms, that may be included within the PL/SQL constituting a trigger or Form-Level Procedure.

**Page** – A SQL*Forms object that owns constant text and that is owned by the Form within which it appears. A Page will have a sequential numeric label, and may be viewed by ensuring the presence of at least one field that may be entered by the cursor. (See also **Cursor (4)**.) Pages may take any size from one screen column by one screen row, up to 255 screen columns by 255 screen rows. Normally, pages are set to the default display size defined for a given operating platform. Additionally, a 'pop-up' attribute may be set for a page, together with various sizing and positioning attributes, that may make it appear as though it were a window opening on top of an existing page. Horizontal and vertical scroll bars and a title may be specified for the virtual pop-up page.

**PL/SQL** – A procedural Oracle programming language (or 'software technology') based upon the US Military implementation of the Ada language. PL/SQL relies upon the inclusion of Structured Query Language statements to return and process information from the Oracle relational database management system with which it will be associated. PL/SQL may be embedded in tools such as SQL*Forms and SQL*ReportWriter (version 2.0); used with Pro*Oracle languages such as Pro*C and Pro*COBOL to enhance productivity; or written in the form of an interpreted language for use with the SQL*PLUS enhanced version of ANSI/ISO SQL provided by Oracle Corporation. The language can use standard SQL functions, features iterative, conditional, directive, recursive, and traditionally procedural elements, and supports the definition of local and global variables on a modular basis. PL/SQL cannot be used as a standalone programming language.

**Pop-up page** – A SQL*Forms Page object for which attributes have been set such that it may appear superimposed upon the preceding display page (screen) as though it had 'popped' up upon it. (See also **Page**.)

**Propagation (exceptions)** – The mechanism by which an exception raised in a PL/SQL sub-block passes out to that block's enclosing block if the exception cannot map to a pre-defined 'Exception Handler' in the EXCEPTION section of that enclosed block. If the enclosing block is the outermost block in the current PL/SQL program and no handler can be found for the exception, control will pass out of the program and yield an error code and error text indicating the name of the exception that could not be handled.

**Propagation (fields)** – The cascading enabling or disabling of the logically interrelated field attributes affected by the dynamic alteration of one of their number by program control during a SQL*Forms runtime session. For example, the automatic disabling of the 'Queryable', 'Enterable', and 'Updateable' attributes when a field's 'Displayed' attribute is turned off by a packaged procedure in a PL/SQL trigger during a runtime session.

**Query mode** – The SQL*Forms runtime mode in which the operator has pressed the [enter query] function key to ready SQL*Forms for a query. In versions of SQL*Forms up to and including Version 3.0, no trigger step (V2) or PL/SQL trigger or Form-Level Procedure statement (V3) may be executed while a Form is in Query mode, and inter-record navigation functions and validation are disabled until [execute query] has completed operation. Programmed Pop-up Lists of Values will function, though.

**Raise** – Initiate an exception condition during the runtime of a PL/SQL program. Normally, control would pass to the Exception Handler defined with the name of the given exception, and the sequence of statements found there, executed. RAISE is available as a directive statement. (See also **Exception**, **Exception Handler**, and **Propagation (exceptions)**.)

**Record (1)** – The set of column data values that constitute a row in a table as it is held in a SQL*Forms Block. A Record is the SQL*Forms version of a Table's Row, therefore, and is constituted by one or more Fields.

**Record (2)** – A PL/SQL object initialized in the declaration section of a PL/SQL Block using the datatype tablename%ROWTYPE, and based upon the row definition for a given table. PL/SQL records are outside the scope of this book.

**Reference** – The logical copying of a SQL*Forms object from one application into another using the SQL*Forms Copy/Reference Object facility. Because a reference is only a logical copy, if the master object changes, its alterations will ripple through to the referencing applications at runtime. Referencing operates by inserting a series of labels into the specification for a Form that point to the referenced application and object in the SQL*Forms system base tables.

**Region** – An area of field text marked by the operator, using the operator's [select] key, while editing a field at runtime. A region will normally be cut or copied into a text buffer in memory for later pasting.

**Restricted (code or trigger)** – A 'Restricted' V2-Macro or V3-Packaged Procedure is one that could affect the standard SQL*Forms operating behaviours. Restricted Macros or Packaged Procedures may only be entered in Restricted-type triggers, of the appropriate style (V2 or V3). Most of these are key triggers. It is illegal to enter Restricted code in an 'Unrestricted'-type trigger, though usually Unrestricted code can quite happily be included in a Restricted-type trigger.

**Savepoint** – A named subsection marker during a transaction. Names may be up to 30 characters in length. Savepoints are usually set prior to a DML statement in a PL/SQL program that the designer feels may need to be reversed under some conditions. A transaction may be rolled back to a savepoint (using ROLLBACK WORK TO savepoint_name command) as many times as necessary. There may be a maximum of five Savepoints per transaction normally or, by arrangement with the DBA, up to 255 per transaction (this must be set before the given Oracle instance is started, since it affects the whole installation). Savepoints exist for the complete transaction until a COMMIT or ROLLBACK, at which point they vanish.

**Scroll bar** – A horizontal or vertical bar at the lowest and leftmost screen rows on screen or in a window. Usually operated by a mouse pointer, it will control the scrolling of the display up, down, left, or right. Although present in Character Mode and Block Mode SQL*Forms installations, scroll bars cannot usually be used, and are included for display compatibility with bitmapped installations. (Always check with the site DBA to ascertain the availability of elements such as scroll bars on your platform.) They are a convention of GUI-type systems. (See **GUI**.)

**Spread Table** – A SQL*Forms display orientation that shows a range of objects arranged horizontally in relation to one another, as though contained in a table, for a defined scope (for example, all the Fields in a Block; all the Blocks in a Form). Spread Tables are useful because they allow the designer to appreciate relative ranges of settings within a given scope.

**SQL** – Structured Query Language. Also known as 'Sequel'. A non-procedural Fourth Generation Language arising from the theoretical work of Dr Ted Codd, and others, in the early 1970s. SQL has two major sublanguages, **DDL** and **DML** (see above), and also elements for establishing and controlling user accounts. SQL has become established as the most famous and widely used database query and programming language, not least because it is available as a tool for use with very many different DBMS products. SQL can be embedded within third-generation languages such as COBOL and Fortran, in the form of ESQL, or Embedded Structured Query Language, and can be used within PL/SQL, Oracle's procedural transaction-processing language.

**Step** – A sequential code element within a SQL*Forms V2-Style Trigger. A step can be composed of one SQL command, or one or more V2 Macros, separated by semi-colons. Each Step has a series of attributes that relate to the processing that takes place as a result of 'Success' and 'Failure' execution status. Steps may also have labels of up to 30 characters length. It is illegal to use PL/SQL in a V2-Style Trigger step.

**Sub-Event** – A moment in SQL*Forms processing time that occurs after exit from an object and before entry to an object. Its occurrence will fire any Trigger code associated with it at the level defined. Effectively, therefore, a Sub-Event will be sparked by the movement of the Navigation Unit as it navigates between objects. (See **Cursor(4)**, **Navigation Unit**.)

**Success** – A technical SQL*Forms status, defined as normally occurring in an executing V2-Style Trigger when one of the following occurs: (1) an SQL DML statement acts upon at least one table row; (2) a V2-Style Trigger step contains no syntax errors; (3) a V2-Style macro executes properly. (See also **Step** and **Failure**.)

**System Variable** – A pre-defined SQL*Forms variable containing a datum indicating a runtime status or condition. All but two of the SQL*Forms system variables (message_level, and suppress_working) cannot be changed by the programmer, since they are used to enable the Forms runtime environment to operate correctly. System variable names are up to 30 characters in length, and are preceded by the word SYSTEM and a full stop.

**Transaction** – Also known as a 'Commit Unit': the group of events that occur between one time and the next time that a user connects to Oracle, disconnects from Oracle, commits DML adjustments to the database, or rolls back DML adjustments.

**Trigger** – A SQL*Forms object or Oracle7 object that contains one or more lines of program code executed sequentially upon the occurrence of a given event in runtime processing. In SQL*Forms, a trigger may be written as either a 'V2-Style Trigger' or a 'V3-Style Trigger'. There are three types of trigger: Key-related, User-Named, and Event-related. Roughly, Key-related triggers are all named after the pre-defined operator function keys available in SQL*Forms; User-Named triggers may take any name defined by the designer, of up to 30 characters; Event-related triggers will all take names of pre-defined events that will be brought to life by the movement of the Navigation Unit as it traverses a running Form. They all have the prefix PRE-, ON-, or POST-, and the name of the pre-defined event. Triggers will belong to a SQL*Forms object, Form, Block, or

Field, and their ownership will determine with what frequency and under what condition they are executed. (See also **Trigger precedence**, **Navigation Unit**, **Cursor**, **Step**, **Success**, **Failure**.)

**Trigger precedence** – So that the designer may make use of identically named triggers, and may determine at what point a trigger is executed, an order of execution precedence has been established in SQL*Forms such that any Field-Level trigger takes precedence over any Block-Level trigger, which takes precedence over any Form-Level trigger of the same name: Field over Block over Form. 'Level' is the scope within which a trigger of a given name is owned. (See also **Trigger**, **Navigation Unit**, **Cursor(4)**.)

**Unrestricted (code or trigger)** – An 'Unrestricted' V2-Macro or V3-Packaged Procedure will not affect the standard SQL*Forms operating behaviours. Unrestricted Macros or Packaged Procedures may be entered in any Unrestricted-type trigger of the appropriate style (V2 or V3), and in 'Restricted'-type triggers. It is illegal to enter Restricted code in an Unrestricted-type trigger.

**User Exit** – A designer-specified call to a program written in a Pro*Oracle language, such as Pro*C or Pro*COBOL. The program will run until it determines, then control will return to the calling application (SQL*Forms, for example).

**User-Named trigger** – A 'V2-Style' or 'V3-Style' Trigger with a name other than an event-related name, of up to 30 characters in length. User-Named triggers must be invoked from Form-Level Procedures or from Event-related triggers (Pre-, On-, or Post-Event).

**V2-Style Trigger** – A trigger containing one or more sequentially executed Steps, each of one or more lines of program code written in SQL or SQL*Forms V2 Macro language. V2-Style Triggers cannot contain PL/SQL code. Each Step may force program control to jump to another Step, or adjust the sequence of processing by using the concepts of Success and Failure.

**V3-Style Trigger** – A trigger containing one or more lines of sequentially executed PL/SQL code. V3-Style Triggers adjust the flow of program control by using logical conditional constructs, rather than by using the concepts of Success and Failure found in 'V2-Style' trigger Steps. V3-Style Triggers may not contain V2-Style Macro code.

**Wigwam symbol** – Not a formal Oracle Corporation technical term, 'Wigwam symbols' is the informal name given to the markers placed around label names in PL/SQL code (thus <<*label*>>) in this book. (See also **Label**.)

# INDEX


% ROWTYPE, *xviii*
% TYPE, 21–22
3GL, 3, 151
4GL, 3, 151

Active set:
  defined, 35, 152
  example, 36
Ada, 10
Anonymous Block:
  defined, 152
  discussion of, 14, 28
Automatic Search and Complete (ASC), 152

Base Table, 152
BEGIN, 12–13
Block:
  byte data (hard disk), 152
  PL/SQL:
    defined, 12, 152
    discussion, 12
  SQL *Forms:
    attributes, 114
    Copy/Reference Object, 122
    defined, 152
    level, 80, 81
    referencing, 108, 121
Block Mode, 81, 153
Blue Wardrobe, 153
Boole, George, 153
Boolean:
  datatype, 20, 35, 73
  defined, 153
  usage, 21

Cha-Cha:
  defined, 153
  discussed, 111
CHAR datatype, 20, 35, 73, 111
Character Mode, 153
Check Box:
  defined, 154
  example, 100
Codd, Dr. Edward (Ted), 162
Commit unit, (*see also* Transaction):
  defined, 154
Compiler:
  defined, 154
  SQL *Forms, 28
Conditional:
  defined, 154
  in PL/SQL, 10, 44, 47–48, 49, 58, 59
Constant:
  datatypes, 20–21
  defined, 154
  usage, 21
Context Area, 154
Control Block, 154
Copy/Reference Object, 29, 122
Cursor, (*see also* Navigation Unit):
  Explicit (PL/SQL):
    and CLOSE, 36
    and Designer's notebook, 37
    and OPEN, 35, 36
    and table columns, 35
    attributes of, 40
    defined, 155
    discussed, 32
    parameterized, 33, 34–36
    pre-defined exception, 62
    rules for using, 34, 35
    simple, 33–34
    testing, 62
  Implicit (SQL):
    attributes of, 40

defined, 154
discussion, 40–42
in Random Access Memory (RAM), 154
SQL*Forms Object:
defined, 155
testing, 112–116
Visual Display Unit (VDU), 155

Data Definition Language (DDL), *xvii*, 155
Date, Chris, 9
DECLARE, 12–13, 19, 20, 21, 30, 46, 52, 57, 70
Dialogue (or Dialog) box:
defined, 155
example, 100
Directive (*see also* RAISE, GOTO):
defined, 155
jumping to labels, 50, 61
Data Manipulation Language (DML):
and batch files in SQL*Plus, 11, 108, 141
and COMMIT, 88, 90, 91, 139, 142
and Commit Unit, 135–143
and PL/SQL, *xviii*, 135–143
and POST, 88
and 'printing' with, 135
and ROLLBACK, 89, 139
and SAVEPOINT, 86, 140
and Transaction, 135–143
defined, 155
DELETE keyword, 16, 138
examples, 135–143
in SQL*Forms Triggers, 80–81, 88–90
INSERT keyword, 135–137
rules for use in PL/SQL, 136
SELECT keyword, 10, 22, 23, 33, 41, 80, 135
SELECT . . . INTO, 22–23
UPDATE keyword, 137
Dongle, 155
DUAL, 10, 144, 155

ELSE, 47, 49
ELSIF, 47, 49
END, 12, 14
END IF, 47, 49
END LOOP, 43, 45
Exception:
defined, 156
designer-defined, 56
discussion, 12–13, 56
examples, 58, 59
handler, 61
in Form-Level Procedure, 69, 72
pre-defined, 61, 62
propagation, 61
raising, 57
rules, 60
section, 12, 58, 69, 72
Exception Handler, 61
EXIT, 43
Explicit Cursor (*see* Cursor, Explicit (PL/SQL)
Explicit Lock, (*see* Lock)

Failure:
defined, 113–114, 156
form_trigger_failure (exception), 62
Packaged Function, 113
trapping, 57, 114, 116
FETCH, 38–40
Field:
SQL*Forms,
attributes, 116
and attribute propagation, 95, 160
and Block Mode, 81
and EDIT_FIELD, 95
and pop-up, 95
assigning value to, 23, 25, 71, 74, 92
clearing, 91
Copy/Reference Object, 122
defined, 17, 156
listing values for, 110
referencing, 17, 108
setting attributes of, 93, 94
testing attributes of, 115
with NAME_IN, 121–122
PL/SQL record, 156
Form:
display mode, 27, 69, 157
SQL*Form (*see* SQL*Forms)
Form-Level Function, 157
Form-Level Procedure:
code syntax of PL/SQL, 69
Copy/Reference Object, 122
definition, 68
examples, 70, 71, 72, 74
invocation of, 69, 71, 74
local variables in, 70
parameterized, 72
simple, 69
FOR loop, 45–47, 103
Forward references, 21

GLOBAL variable:
assigning a value to, 16, 23, 25, 40, 59, 70–72, 92
attributes of, 16

defined, 16, 19
erasing, 104
GOTO, 50
Graphical User Interface (GUI), 157

Identifiers, PL/SQL, 19
IF, 47
Implicit Cursor, (*see* Cursor, Implicit (SQL))
Implicit Lock (*see* Lock)
Index variable:
as constant, 46
defined, 157
in FOR loop, 45
Indirection:
defined, 158
with NAME_IN, 121–122
Initialization:
defined, 158
of cursors, 35
of variables, 20
Instantiation, 158

Key Trigger, 82, 84–85, 105
Koch, George, 103

Label:
defined, 158
examples, 45, 46, 50
rules for, 51
List of Values (LOV):
and LIST_VALUES, 110
and Query Mode Programming, 161
defined, 158
Lock, 106, 107, 158
LOCK TABLE, 159

Macro, 10, 78, 84–85, 159
Messages, 110, 118–121

Navigation Unit, (*see also* Cursor, SQL *Forms Object):
defined, 159
position of, 18
Null:
and variables, 18, 20
defined, 159
testing for, 44, 48
NUMBER datatype, 20, 35, 73

Object-naming conventions, 15, 20, 24–25, 70, 79
Object Oriented Database Management System (OODBMS), 159
Oracle7, *xix*, 151

Packaged Function:
defined, 159
discussion, 112–122
examples, 113, 114, 118, 120, 121, 122
Packaged Procedure:
and function keys compared, 84–85
and V2-style macros compared, 84–85
defined, 160
discussion, 10, 78–111
invocation of, 78
names of, 83
restricted, 82, 161
unrestricted, 82, 164
Page:
and Copy/Reference Object, 122
and SYNCHRONIZE, 103
attributes of, 99
changing dynamically, 102
coordinates used with, 97
defined, 160
examples, 98, 147–149
philiosophy behind, 96
Parameter, (*see also* Cursor, Parameterized and Form-Level Procedure, Parameterized)
Parallel Universe Limited, *xviii*, 131–134
PL/SQL:
basis for, 10
batch, 11, 15, 108
block, 12, 61, 71
compiling, 28
conditionals, 10, 44, 47, 49, 58–59
defined, 160
discussion, *xvii*, 9–12
embedded, 12
example code, 16, 21–25, 27, 28, 33, 34, 36, 37, 39–40, 43, 45, 46, 49, 50, 58, 60, 63, 70–72, 74, 103–104, 113, 114, 118, 120, 135–143
exceptions, (*see* Exception)
language rules, 14
nested, 13, 14
output, 110–111
sections of, 12–13
syntax in Form-Level Procedures, 69, 72
variables, 17, 19–22, 79
with DML, 135–143
Pop-up page, (*see also* Page):
defined, 160
PRAGMA EXCEPTION_INIT, *xviii*
*Principia Mathematica*, 51
Procedure (*see* Form-Level Procedure)
Propagation (Exceptions):
defined, 160

Propagation (Exceptions) (*continued*)
rules for, 61
Propagation (Fields), (*see also* Field):
defined, 161
setting attributes, 95
testing attributes, 115

Query Mode, 86, 105, 161

RAISE:
defined, 161
discussion, 60
implicit, 62
Record:
in SQL*Forms, 80, 91, 106, 107, 161
in PL/SQL, 161
Reference, 161
Region:
defined, 161–162
COPY, CUT, PASTE, 92
Restricted Code or Trigger:
defined, 161–162
table showing, 80, 83, 83–85

Savepoint:
automatically issued, 86, 89
defined, 140, 162
example, 141
Scroll bar, 162
SELECT:
in Explicit Cursors, 33
in Implicit Cursors, 41
in PL/SQL, 22
in Triggers, 10
INTO clause, 22–23
Sequel, (*see* Structured Query Language (SQL)
Spread Table:
display mode, 162
examples, 27, 68, 100
SQL*Forms:
and SQL*Menu link, 83, 87
and SQL*ReportWriter, 109
Blocks, 152
calling from another Form, 86
calling operating system commands from, 108
calling user-exits from, 109
Copy/Reference Object in, 122–124
defined, 156
errors, 62, 116–118
exiting, 87, 118
fatal errors in, 114
Fields, (*see* Field SQL *Forms)
Form-Level Functions, 157
Form-Level Procedures, (*see* Form-Level Procedure)
GLOBAL variables (*see* GLOBAL variable)
V2-macros in, 10, 84–85, 159
Packaged Functions, 112–122
Packaged Procedures, 78–111
Pages, 96–122
starting Form as new, 87
SYSTEM variables, (*see* SYSTEM variable)
testing characteristics of, 19–112
trapping errors in, 116-118
trapping messages in, 118–121
Trigger types in, 26, 63
SQL*Menu:
error codes for, 117
message codes for, 119
SQL*Plus:
and PL/SQL, 11, 109
batch files, 11, 15
SQL*ReportWriter, using with SQL*Forms, 109
Structured Query Language (SQL):
defined, 162
rules for use in PL/SQL, 22
rules for use in Explicit Cursors, 33–35
relationship to PL/SQL, 9
discussion of, 3, 9
in Triggers, 80–81
Step, 162
Sub-Block, 13
Sub-Event, 163
Success:
defined, 113–114, 162
packaged function, 113
trapping, 57, 114
Symbols, PL/SQL, 15
SYSTEM variable:
assigning a value prohibited, 17
attributes of, 17
defined, 17–19, 163
example, 108
types of, 18

TO_CHAR formatting, 144–146
Transaction:
defined, 163
discussed, 140
Trigger:
calling Form-Level Procedures from, 70–71
Copy/Reference Object, 122

defined, 163
key-related, 82, 84–85, 105
ownership of, 80
restricted, 82, 161
steps of code within, 162
unrestricted, 82, 164
user-named, 81, 82, 164
V2-Style, 84, 164
V3-Style, 14, 26, 28, 164
levels of precedence,
defined, 163
discussion, 81–82
Trigger precedence, 81–82, 163

Unrestricted Code or Trigger:
defined, 164
table showing, 80, 83, 84–85
User Exit:
defined, 164
invocation, 109
User-Named Trigger:
defined, 82, 164
invocation, 85

VARCHAR2 datatype, 20
Variables, PL/SQL, 19–22, 45, 46, 72
V2-Style Trigger, 84, 164
V3-Style Trigger, 14, 26, 28, 63, 103, 164

WHILE, *xviii*
Wigwam symbols, << >>, 15, 164